WITCHCRAFT LEGACY

WITCHCRAFT LEGACY

Stories from the Big Attic

RICHARD WARREN BREWSTER

PROTEAN PRESS
Rockport, Massachusetts

Protean Press
21 Broadway, Suite 5
Rockport, MA 01966
www.ProteanPress.com

ISBN 978-0-9913520-6-7

Credits
Book produced by Open Book Systems, Inc. Text and cover design by Janis Owens. This book was typeset in Adobe Caslon by Janis Owens.

Cover illustration: Handwritten notes by William Stoughton, chief judge of the Salem witchcraft trials, on flyleaf of *Select Discourses* (John Smith, London, 1660).

The following pages are about ancient books that my brother
Sam and I found in a trunk in the attic when we were little kids.
The old tomes once belonged to the chief judge of the 1692
Salem witchcraft trials. I tell stories about people connected
to these old books as they passed from hand to hand from the
witchcraft judge to Sam and me and finally to a book collector in
Connecticut to whom I sold them so that I could buy diamond
studs for my wife, Barbara. This small collection of stories,
covering nearly four centuries, is dedicated to the woman for
whose ears I bought the sparkles.

R.W.B.

Many have fallen since my race begun.
Many will fall ere my race is run.

*On a yellowing piece of paper tacked inside
the door of Aunt Sally's tall case clock*

CONTENTS

PREFACE

Eᴀʀʟɪᴇʀ ɪɴ the week, Barbara and I, locked down in New York City by the Coronavirus, were sharing Zoom cocktails with Cousin Lisa, similarly locked down in Lexington, Virginia. As well as having a cocktail, Lisa was sewing face masks, using a thimble that Mom gave her 65 years ago. We talked about the thimble and I mentioned a few other family memories. Lisa said, "You really should write this stuff down."

There is nothing like a stay-at-home order during a pandemic to give you time to write, so I have taken Lisa's words to heart—she was the voice of my conscience. For a long time, I have been meaning to write down the story of the ancient books that Sam and I found in the attic and the eerie and haunting notes on the back flyleaf of one of those books. The notes crowd the flyleaf in crabbed handwriting penned in ink long since turned brown with age. Below a heading about "extracting" things from someone named Henry Peacham, the first line speaks of "Evil Spirits." Sam and I completely misunderstood both the heading and the notes. We imagined a curse, torture, a forced confession, statements "extracted" from someone named Peacham as he lay on a medieval rack, possibly crucified after he was tortured.

The handwritten notes appear in one of the books, *Select Discourses*, published in London in 1660, the year Oliver Cromwell's head was exhumed and placed on a spike at Westminster Hall to mark the end of Puritan rule and celebrate the return of the monarchy. In 1662, William Stoughton, a Puritan from Massachusetts and the owner of *Select Discourses*, left the inhospitable (for Puritans) environment of Restoration England and returned to a political and moneymaking career in Massachusetts. Thirty years later he presided over the 1692–1693 Salem witchcraft trials.

The ancient tomes and Stoughton's flyleaf notes had an impact on me from the moment Sam and I unearthed them from a steamer trunk in our attic. They also connect me to all the books' owners since the witchcraft judge and to the most important people in my life, including Sam and the rest of the family. I have traced the books as they moved from 1660 to today from one hand to the next, from William Stoughton to Sam and me and beyond. The strange tale of their travels and each of the men and women who owned them over nearly 400 years is told in this book. In the pages that follow I also tell stories about people in my life who are, in one way or another, connected to Stoughton's books and the other ancient papers we found—stories about those people, their life experiences, their humanity and mortality...the rain that falls equally on us all.

For a long time I have intended to write down these things, and the Coronavirus lockdown has given me time. No more excuses. A yellowing piece of paper tacked inside the door of Aunt Sally's tall-case clock has given me a nudge every week when I open the case to stop the pendulum and wind the clock. After I stop the pendulum, I reach up and open the smaller arched door that frames the glass over the clock face. Turning the key in the hole on the right side of the clock face raises a weight below that makes the hour, minute, and second hands continue their circle rounds and tell time for another week. Turning the key in the hole on the left raises the much heavier weight that makes the clock chime. Ingenious gears in the clockworks make the sun and moon rise and set over a ship forever at sea. The sun, moon, and ship appear in a crescent window in the clock face above the dial. If someone remembers to wind it, there is no reason the old clock cannot continue to tell time, chime, and show the rising and setting sun and moon for many years to come.

Inside the door of the clock's case just above the old scrap of paper with the rhyme about time and mortality cited at the beginning of this book, there is a torn jelly-jar label, also brown with age. It says that the clock was Aunt Sally's clock. Aunt Sally was born in what was then called the District of Maine, more than 250 years ago, before the end of the American Revolution. Aunt Sally's clock has been telling time for quite a while.

Relatively speaking, I've been around for quite a while, too. Sometimes it takes a bit of doing for me to turn the keys and raise the heavy weights. I may need to switch hands to finish the job. When both weights are raised to the top of the case, the time can be set and the pendulum can be gently pushed to the side and released to start it swinging again. The strikers for the chimes are wrapped in felt. They toll softly on the hour. The chimes and the strength required to wind the clock are reminders of the urgency to get things done, striking a chord with the words on the yellowing scrap of paper.

My brother Sam was more than two years older than me and died two years ago. I will be 79 this November. So, with Cousin Lisa's urging, I am finally getting down to it. In our small family circle in cyberspace between New York and Virginia, Lisa passed me an eagle feather—a talking piece empowering me to speak.

I have always liked Mark Twain, who apologized for writing a long letter, saying, "I didn't have time to write a short letter." I believe that five words are better than ten and I promise you brevity. If you choose to read this little book, I will give you nearly 400 years of history in fewer than 200 pages. My tales of love and loss, death of some and survival of others, are connected to one family and, in part, are written so that that family's next generation—Sylvia, Scott, Amelie, Darrah, Will, and Charlotta—can read or hear a few stories about people who are gone and times gone by.

I have also written this little book for the world, for anyone who chooses to read it. My stories are about humanity as I have known it and I tell them as honestly as I can.

Richard Warren Brewster
April 12, 2020
In lockdown

CHAPTER I.

Sam and I Find the
Witchcraft Judge's Books
(c. 1951)

Those Evil Spirits haunt me Every Day & will
not let me Eat, Hear, Read or Pray.

William Stoughton's flyleaf note
'Select Discourses', *London 1660*

I WAS 10 and Sam was 12 at the end of 1951. I can't put an exact date on it, but at about that time Sam and I found the books that had once been owned by William Stoughton, chief judge of the 1692–1693 Salem witchcraft trials. One of the books is a compilation, *Select Discourses* on various subjects, including the Devil. The book has creepy flyleaf notations handwritten by Stoughton, including the one quoted at the top of this page.

Sam and I were often unsupervised in those days, as Pop was in and out of hospitals and Mom ran the automobile business when Pop was away. Our sister, Isabel, 20, and brother, Tom, 18, had left the Glen Cove nest. Left to our own devices, Sam and I had opportunity and space for the creative design of our activities. Sam was the leader in coming up with things to do—like shooting a flaming arrow through the hornets' nest hanging from one of the old maple trees near the columned porch off the big room at the west end of the house.

Sam's plan started in the flower pantry between the main dining room and the maids' dining room. On shelves above the flower-pantry sink was a collection of vases, as well as hurricane lamps filled with kerosene, ready for emergencies when we lost electricity. Next to the sink were drawers with pruning shears, twine, and a collection of rags. We tied a rag onto the end of one of our target arrows and drenched it in kerosene from a hurricane lamp. Then, armed with our 30-lb bow and a box of kitchen matches, we headed out the dining room's French doors and followed the terrace until we reached the end porch.

The bow was pale yellow, a traditional English long bow made of yew wood. Sam and I often spent time together shooting arrows at the straw target on the lawn below the terrace, imagining we were in Sherwood Forest. Sam was stronger and more skilled with the bow and so, in our hornets' nest caper, he was the designated archer. He notched the fateful arrow on the bowstring as we approached the nest. I had the matches. About 20 feet from the nest, Sam gave the command, "Light the damned arrow, stupid!" I fumbled with the matches, struck one, and lit the kerosene-soaked rag. It immediately became a ball of flame. Sam drew the bow. Its yellow shaft bent as he reached full draw with the feathered fletching of the arrow at the corner of his mouth, just as we imagined an archer did in Sherwood Forest. The flaming rags at the other end of the arrow were uncomfortably close to Sam's left hand. He released the bowstring. The arrow flew. It hurtled through the 20 feet of air above the lawn and smashed into the hornets' nest. Not pleased, the hornets came swarming out of the shattered nest. In a fury they flew by the regiment in our direction. As Sam let fly the flaming arrow, I had placed myself behind him and was able to run fast enough to get through one of the two screen doors between the end porch and the living room before the hornets got to me.

Sam was a few steps behind me and several of the hornets stung him before he made it to safety.

The house where these things happened was a big house, about 35 rooms. In fact, everyone who worked in the house as well as the gardeners who worked on the property called it the "Big House," not that it had any connection to Sing Sing penitentiary up the Hudson, also called the Big House. Instead, the house where Sam and I lived was called the Big House to distinguish it from the two cottages on the east side of the apple orchard, past the chicken coop, and close to Crescent Beach Road. The East Cottage was where the gardener, Peter Renaldo, and his family lived above a garage, horse stable, and the potato cellar in the hillside. The West Cottage was where another gardener or the coachman (later the chauffeur) used to live. When Sam and I were little kids, Mom and Pop rented out the West Cottage, and for two summers we lived in it when the Big House was rented out. Across the back drive from the East Cottage was a path to the vegetable gardens, potting shed, cold frames, and a long greenhouse with curved glass where Mom had raised orchids before I was born.

The grounds were about four acres, not huge, but enough to keep Peter Renaldo busy. There was a chicken coop between the orchard and the West Cottage, which, along with the vegetable garden, was part of Pop's idea that "the boys should learn where food came from." Sam and I watched as Peter cut the heads off the old chickens in the garage yard. We watched the chickens literally run around the yard with their heads cut off. Mom made casseroles out of the decapitated chickens, which she called "old hens with a new look," meaning that she used slow cooking to tenderize the old birds' tough meat.

The chicken coop, with the younger egg-producing hens, kept Sam busy after school until he went away to boarding school.

After that, I took over the egg collecting, often with an imaginary monster behind me as I raced with the eggs in a wire basket to the back door of the Big House in the dark after school.

When Grandmother and Grandfather Brewster bought the place in 1902 after Pop was born, they came out to Glen Cove from their townhouse at 49th Street and Fifth Avenue in their carriage, which their coachman Frederick drove over the Queensboro Bridge and out Route 25A to Long Island. Soon after they moved into the house in Glen Cove, one of the neighbors, Mrs. Pratt, said to my grandmother, "Isabel, you are lucky you have a small place to manage." The Pratt homes, farther down Crescent Beach Road and on nearby Dosoris Lane, sat on hundreds of acres straddling both Glen Cove and neighboring Lattingtown. The Pratt mansions did, indeed, make our 35-room house look small.

But by any normal standard, our house was huge. The living room, known to all as the "big room," was off limits to Sam and me unless we had permission or when the doors were opened for Christmas Eve, Christmas Day, or another special occasion. Just inside, behind the closed doors that separated the big room from the front hall, were the snarling heads, ferocious teeth and increasingly moth-eaten skins of three tigers that Pop had shot for bounty for the French government in 1923, about 30 miles from Saigon. Past the tigers, the big room was filled with 18th-century furniture from the family house in Wiscasset, Maine, from which the books of the witchcraft judge had also made their way to Glen Cove.

On the walls of the big room were large portraits, including two by van Dyck, which Pop later sold to postpone moving from the Big House to the poor house. Over the fireplace between the screen doors to the end porch, there was a large portrait of Mom in a dark red velvet dress done by a portrait artist named Gerald Brockhurst. He had caught Mom's beauty, but made her seem

4

remote, severe, and critical. I understand what he may have seen—she could, at times, be distant and made me long for her approval. Never warm and fuzzy, Mom expressed her love in other ways.

The big room was so-called to distinguish it from the room across the front hall. That room we called "the library," because it had bookshelves with the works of Mark Twain, Kipling, and James Fenimore Cooper as well as the *Encyclopedia Britannica*, all of which my grandfather, "Gramps" to me, dipped into and read to us when he and my grandmother, "Omy" (Mom's parents), came to stay. The library was our real living room. There was also a radio on the bookshelves, turned on so that Mom, Pop, Omy, and Gramps could listen to the evening news. Pop's parents, Grandmother and Grandfather Brewster, had also sat in the same library, but they both died long before my time.

Sam and I were, in theory, seen and not heard, and in the library before dinner the grown-ups sipped a Manhattan with a Maraschino cherry (Omy and Gramps), more than one martini (Pop), and a glass of Dubonnet (Mom), while Mom worked on a square for a needlepoint rug. When all the squares were done, the needlepoint rug would eventually show the three tigers that Pop shot in 1923. Before or after the news, Gramps would help Sam and me with our scrapbooks or read something amazing to us from the *Encyclopedia Britannica* or a story about the adventures of Mowgli or the Connecticut Yankee.

On the third floor of the house, there were six maids' rooms where the household staff of eight maids and a butler lived before Grandmother Brewster died and Mom and Pop moved into the house in 1939. I was told that Pop let the butler go, not because he was worried about money at that point, but because he didn't like anyone opening the door for him. By the time I came along the family had only day help. No one lived on the third floor except, for a while, Olga and Blanca, young Ecuadorian maids who lived there for a few years and made unforgettable chicken tamales steamed in cornhusks.

On the south side of the third floor, between the maids' and butler's rooms, was the "little attic"—a cluttered room with built-in drawers overflowing with framed family pictures and albums. Across the hall on the north side was the "big attic." There was a large cedar closet on the left as you entered and just beyond, the big attic opened onto a vast sea of steamer trunks lying in north-south rows from one side of the room to the other. Their dark shapes were like coffins in which the family's past was buried and in between the rows were shadowy corridors where Sam and I could crawl and hide.

Inside the trunks were endless amazing things for us to examine—military uniforms worn by Uncle Sydney and Gramps in the First World War, riding clothes and riding crops, fur lap robes for carriages or open automobiles and more. One of the trunks was filled with 17th- and 18th-century books and family papers from the house in Wiscasset into which Grandmother Brewster's family had moved in 1760. (The house's first owner had been tomahawked near the end of the Seven Years' War, or the part of that war that came to an end in North America when the British defeated the French on the Plains of Abraham in Quebec. British victory in Quebec made the part of Massachusetts called "the District of Maine" and Wiscasset, the village where our house was located, a safe place for British colonists to settle.)

One day Sam and I delved into the family letters and old books. One by one, we lifted the packets of letters, ledgers, and ancient books from the trunk. Most were boring to 10- and 12-year-old boys, but then we found several books at least 100 years older than the next oldest book. These books were leather-bound, which gave them an eerie and ancient appearance, and were printed in London or Cambridge between 1652 and 1660. A name, William Stoughton, was handwritten at the top of the front flyleaf. We had no clue who he was.

Sam and I did not then know that we were looking at the same signature that appeared on the death warrants for Salem "witches." Nor did we know that those death sentences were brought about, in large part, because Chief Judge Stoughton ruled that "spectral evidence," such as a witness's dreams, visions, and ravings, could be introduced to prove that a woman was a witch.

The titles and sub-titles of Stoughton's religious tomes were mostly lost on Sam and me, though we could see that they dealt with things like battles with Satan. We took the ancient books to the center of the big attic for a closer look under the light bulb that hung there on an electrical cord from the ceiling. In the volume dealing with Satan, we saw notations crammed onto the rear flyleaf in meticulous, crabbed handwriting indistinguishable from the William Stoughton signature on the book's front flyleaf. Most of the notations were indecipherable to us. What little we could make out was fearful, ominous. At the top of the flyleaf was a heading stating that the material below was "Extracted Out of Mr. Henry Peacham o/c:"

"What does *extracted* mean?" I asked Sam, because he usually knew things I didn't.

Sam scowled at his idiot little brother, "How do you think they extracted things out of people in those days?" Images of the rack, whips, and chains flooded my brain as I thought of the unfortunate Peacham.

"What does the *o/c* mean?" I asked.

"It could mean 'on the cross.' Maybe they crucified him after they tortured him."

Immediately below this scary heading we could make out only the first seven words "extracted" from Henry Peacham's tortured soul:

"Those Evil Spirits haunt me Every Day…"

Neither of us had the ability or attention span to decipher any more of the antique script that filled the page below.

At the time of our discovery, Sam and I thought that the "Evil Spirits" referred to some ancient curse. The "evil spirits" that haunted Henry Peacham, that would not let him eat, hear, read, or pray were noted, by hand, in a family book, in the family's steamer trunk, in the family's attic, and had come from the family's homestead in Maine. To me, the curse was undoubtedly connected to the family. Maybe it explained why Pop had been paralyzed by what Mom called a "stroke" after the war, when he was in his mid 40s. Maybe the curse had to do with the shakes and twitches that he sometimes had or with his trips to hospitals that left Mom to run the business.

Over the course of a rainy winter in Manhattan a half century later, and after corresponding and working with an archivist at Oxford, where Stoughton did graduate work in the 1650s and, indeed, purchased the books that Sam and I found, I learned the true meaning of his flyleaf notes: The lines beginning "Those Evil Spirits haunt me Every Day" were excerpts from a Jacobean poem by Thomas Randolph, railing in fury at the bill collectors and creditors who were beating down his door to collect their money. The rest were random notes of Stoughton's thoughts and excerpts from a book called *The Worth Of A Penny, Or A Caution To Keep Money*, by Henry Peacham, first published in 1641, before William Stoughton traveled from Massachusetts to England.

My older—and wiser—brother and I were wrong. "Extracted out of Mr. Henry Peacham" did not mean a confession extracted out of Peacham by torture! Stoughton was merely referencing literary extracts or excerpts, gems of money-making advice that Stoughton, obsessed with money, culled from Peacham's book and wrote down, along with his own bizarre arithmetic calculations showing how he could work and save, turning pennies, shillings, and pounds into a fortune.

But such knowledge came to me later in life. As a 10-year-old boy I knew the "Evil Spirits" to be some Brewster family curse, which the tortured Peacham had screamed out from the dark days of the New England witchcraft trials. Real or not, the family curse, fueled by my life experiences, stayed tucked away somewhere in my own spiritual attic.

CHAPTER 2.

The Chicken Murders —
A Story of Providence and Provenance
(1650–1799)

> [W]hom hath the Lord more signally exalted
> than his people in this Wilderness...God
> hath sifted a whole Nation that he might send
> Choice Grain over into this Wilderness.
>
> *William Stoughton,*
> *April 29, 1669*

Providence (with a capital "P") is God's divine plan. Provenance, on the other hand, deals with the worldly question of where an object comes from. For art or antique dealers, provenance authenticates a piece by tracing it from the hands of the artist or original owner to the present day.

In the quote at the beginning of this chapter William Stoughton is speaking of divine Providence. The Puritans were chosen by God to populate the desolate wilderness of North America, which had recently been depopulated by what King James I described as "a wonderful plague." Transmitted to natives by European traders, fishermen, and explorers, the plague wiped out much of the indigenous population in the decade just before English settlement began in earnest in 1620. The English settlers found cleared fields and desolate villages emptied by disease. In today's lights the

Providential vision of the 1660s does not seem so exalted, nor the plague so wonderful.

I turn from divine Providence to mundane provenance and briefly trace the movement of the books that Sam and I found as they passed from hand to hand from 1660 until 1801, when they came into our family. Until 2003, two years after Mom died, I thought nothing of the books' provenance nor of their original owners in the 1600s. At the time of Mom's death, Sam and I were the only ones interested in the ancient books. We talked about it. Sam took one of them and I took three, including *Select Discourses*.

Over a rainy weekend in Manhattan, in the winter of 2003, I decided to do an Internet search of the name William Stoughton, which appeared at the top of the front flyleaf on each of the 17th-century tomes. My search quickly led to the Salem witchcraft trials. At my laptop, I stared at the signature of William Stoughton on death warrants for witches in the 1690s. I looked at the Stoughton signatures in my ancient books. They matched. But how did his books come to be in my family's possession?

The long and short of the old books' provenance is that they passed through four owners before they were acquired by our many-times-great-grandfather, Freeman Parker. Those four previous owners were William Stoughton, John Danforth, Reverend Jonathan Bowman, and his son, Squire Jonathan Bowman.

Most of what I know about William Stoughton, the books' first owner, comes from his handwritten notations on the flyleaf of *Select Discourses*, published in 1660. Oliver Cromwell had died two years earlier and, in 1660, his Puritan Commonwealth was overthrown. The English monarchy was restored and Cromwell's body was exhumed from the grave, his head placed on a spike at Westminster Hall to rot in public view.

Nor were things going well for William Stoughton. He had returned to England from Massachusetts in 1650 after graduating from Harvard that same year. Cromwell was then in power and it was a good time for a Puritan from Massachusetts to travel to England. Stoughton received a graduate degree in divinity from New College, Oxford, in 1653 and intended to spend the rest of his life as a minister, most likely in England. But his hopes were dashed in 1660 with the restoration of the monarchy. Stoughton was already 30 and well into a career as a minister. But the now well-established Puritan preacher lost both his paying Oxford fellowship and his job as a minister in Sussex. He was far away from family support in Massachusetts.

With no job, Stoughton must have struggled to pay his bills until he returned to America in 1662. Small wonder, then, that the poem, "On Importunate Duns" by Thomas Randolph—from which Stoughton copied at length onto the flyleaf of *Select Discourses*—resonated with the unemployed minister. The piece, after all, tells of the despised bill-collectors trying to break down the door of the poet who cannot pay his bills.

Stoughton's extract begins:

Those Evil Spirits haunt me Every Day & will not let me Eat, Hear, Read or Pray.

It must have struck a powerful chord. Stoughton *verbatim* copied down 16 lines from Randolph's diatribe, including the following:

I cannot, will not, nay ought not pay.
You are Extortioners. I was not Sent
To Increase your Sins, but to make you all Repent
That er'e you trusted me.
Where my poor Stomach barks for meat, I Dare

Scarce humour it; They make me live by Air
As the Chameleons do.

In counterpoint with Randolph's poem on penniless starvation, the rest of Stoughton's notes are a collection of extracts from and references to Henry Peacham's *The Worth Of A Penny*, a small treatise on how to make and keep money, plus Stoughton's own handwritten notes on how to build a fortune from pennies, then shillings, then pounds. Next to his obsessive notes about money-making, Stoughton repeatedly penned: "Mem. Mem. Mem." for the Latin command *Memini*: "Remember this. Remember this. Remember this."

William Stoughton may or may not have seen Cromwell's head on the spike at Westminster Abbey, but he saw how a preacher could lose his job, become penniless, and be hounded by bill collectors when the political winds shifted in a country or parish. He became determined to make money, even to build a fortune. And he would avoid anything that could get in the way of his goal. Echoing Peacham, he noted on the flyleaf of *Select Discourses* that women, in particular, wasted a man's money through "high living, idlenesse, wastfullnesse, furbelowed Scarves & scolding [their husbands] from Home." (I am not sure what "furbelowed Scarves" are but they sound expensive.)

In 1662, Stoughton returned to Massachusetts. He was offered a job as a pastor in Dorchester, Massachusetts, but turned it down. Indeed, he turned his back on the ministry for good and, for the rest of his life, pursued money and power. He achieved both and never lost his grip on either.

William Stoughton became one of the richest—if not *the* richest—men in Massachusetts, as well as one of the most powerful. He rose to become lieutenant governor and acting governor of the Colony, and chief judge of the witchcraft trials, where his bizarre rulings admitting evidence of dreams and visions would ultimately lead to the death of 20 "witches," most of them women. Hardly alone in the 17th century, Stoughton believed in Satanic possession. The pages of *Select Discourses* that deal with the Devil transforming people into "foul Fiends of darkness" were dog-eared. The combination of his 17th-century belief in Satanic possession and misogyny made Stoughton the monster of the Salem witchcraft trials.

He was a disagreeable man, called the "atrabilious bachelor" by many of his contemporaries. His woman-hating and money-obsessed notes fill the flyleaf of his book. Was Stoughton himself a "Fiend of darkness" with no redeeming human qualities? He did have a few friends. His fellow witchcraft judge, Sam Sewall, for one, stood by him.

Some people like Stoughton never admit error and never repent even their most heinous wrongs. The convictions and subsequent deaths of the innocent women and men of Salem would not have occurred without Stoughton. Yet he never expressed regret. Sam Sewall did. Indeed, Sewall went on to advocate against slavery—the first person in America to publicly take a moral position against the practice. Nevertheless, long after the trials, Sewall continued to visit his old friend Stoughton in Dorchester. When Sewall called at William Stoughton's farm, Stoughton did not offer his friend wine or whiskey, but served hot chocolate with venison, prompting Sewall to say, "Massachusetts and Mexico meet at Your Honor's table."

Sewall and Stoughton shared a love of Harvard. Stoughton was that growing institution's greatest benefactor in the 17th century. In 1698 he was the first person to give Harvard a building, Stoughton Hall. Several years later, at the 1701 Harvard graduation in Cambridge, as Stoughton lay dying in Dorchester,

Sam Sewall presented the college, on his dying friend's behalf, with a 10-inch-high ceremonial communal grace cup made by Boston's greatest silversmith, John Coney, designer of Harvard's seal. The "Stoughton Cup" remains a treasure to this day, on loan by Harvard to the Fogg Museum.

Stoughton died a week after the 1701 graduation. To fund scholarships for future students, he left valuable land holdings to Harvard, which he considered a blessing to the "people of God in this wilderness." He specified that scholarships would favor students from his hometown of Dorchester, neighboring towns, and Native Americans. His will provided that several rooms at Stoughton Hall must be available to Native American students *gratis*. William Stoughton scholarships still fund Harvard students today. Stoughton also created separate funds for education and assistance to the poor in Dorchester and neighboring towns. Nor did he forget those individuals who had been important to him: in his will he left substantial property and money to a nephew, to his housekeeper, and to a doorman at Harvard College.

William Stoughton's vision of the future included Native Americans. Yet he may not have clearly perceived that the continent would be seeded with multi-colored "Choice Grains" growing into the diverse, sometimes deeply divided, sometimes united people on a continent where he and his fellow Puritans once saw only wilderness.

With few friends, William Stoughton lived alone. He never married. The inscription on his tomb describes his erudition and achievements but notes that he was a "man of wedlock unknown."

And the books? They passed from Stoughton to John Danforth following Stoughton's return to Massachusetts in 1662. Danforth was another close friend of Stoughton, though much younger. He was clearly delighted and honored to have the books and, next to the 1660 publication date on the title page of *Select Discourses*, he noted "*Anno nativitatis* John Danforth" (John Danforth's year of birth)—he was three decades younger than his mentor. Stoughton inscribed Danforth's name immediately below his own on the front flyleaf.

Danforth graduated from Harvard in 1677, more than a quarter century after Stoughton. He was then ordained as a minister and got the job that Stoughton had once turned down—minister of the church in Dorchester. For the rest of his life, from 1682 to 1729, Danforth worked as minister of the Dorchester church. He married and he and his wife, Elizabeth, had 12 children. They named one Israel Stoughton Danforth and another Stoughton Danforth.

Danforth died in 1730, eight years after his wife and almost 30 years after Stoughton. In a bizarre final sign of his attachment to the older man, Danforth was buried in the tomb of William Stoughton.

After Danforth's death, Stoughton's books moved into the hands of the new pastor of the Dorchester church, Jonathan Bowman. And now, in a bizarre episode, chickens enter the story.

The Reverend Bowman became minister of the Dorchester Church in 1729, when John Danforth was too ill to continue. Like his predecessor, Bowman remained minister of the church for decades, until things took a bad turn in the 1770s. The by-now-elderly minister acquired a small flock of pet hens. He enjoyed their eggs and kept the birds in the yard of the parish house where he lived. Reverend Bowman loved his hens, but they repeatedly wandered onto the property of a church parishioner and Dorchester neighbor, Paul Hill. Hill objected to the chicken droppings on his front doorsteps and one day, perhaps slipping on chicken manure as he entered or left his home, Hill lost his temper, loaded his blunderbuss, and shot and killed the reverend's hens.

Reverend Bowman's 43-year ministry at the church crumbled. He could not forgive Hill's slaughter of his chickens and refused to baptize Hill's child. This led to a rift between Bowman and his entire congregation. The last straw came when the reverend delivered a personal attack from his pulpit against a number of parishioners, including the slayer of his beloved hens. Perhaps Bowman was suffering from dementia, but whatever the reasons for his behavior, in 1772 the parish fired him after four decades of service.

Reverend Bowman's son, Squire Jonathan Bowman, had moved to frontier Maine in 1760 and for the last three years of his life, Reverend Bowman lived with him there. He took with him his library of religious works—including the Stoughton books brought from England in 1662.

The ministry was not for the reverend's son. Instead, Squire Bowman had become a flourishing entrepreneur with interests in Wiscasset and Dresden, Maine. He acquired a brewery, flour mills, wharves, stores, and was a real-estate developer. In Dresden, church services and judicial proceedings had been held in a fort at least since the 1760s, but in 1800 a new Congregational church was being built and Squire Bowman took the lead in finding a minister.

At the time, my many-times-great-grandfather, Freeman Parker, was seeking work as a minister. He had received a degree in divinity from Harvard in the 1790s and expressed strong interest in the position at the new church in Dresden. He and Bowman corresponded. In the fall of 1800, Freeman Parker traveled from his family's home in Barnstable, Massachusetts, to Dresden to meet with Squire Bowman and others. As Parker proudly wrote to his mother after the successful interview, the $500 annual salary he was offered was "the largest salary...offered to any clergyman in the district of Maine," except for a minister in Kennebunk, whose annual salary was $20 more. Freeman Parker was ordained as minister of the church in Dresden on September 2, 1801.

Squire Bowman, who had no interest in religious works, gave his long-dead father's library of religious volumes, including William Stoughton's books, to Freeman Parker. And, when Freeman Parker died more than 50 years later, in 1854, those books were in the inventory of his estate.

So it was that, thanks to a chain of providential or fortuitous events, not the least of which was the murder of a flock of chickens in 1770, Sam and I found strange treasure in a steamer trunk in the attic in Glen Cove—the inventory of Freeman Parker's estate, neatly bundled family correspondence and papers dating back centuries, the four 17th-century books once owned by William Stoughton, and many 18th-century and 19th-century volumes later acquired by John Danforth, Reverend Bowman, and Freeman Parker.

CHAPTER 3.

Rebecca, Freeman, and the Parker Girls
(1799–1899)

> Let not the thought of Death be ever out of
> your mind.
>
> *Letter from Rebecca Kingsbury Rice*
> *to her daughter, Rebecca.*
> *June 5, 1797*

In 1781 Freeman Parker's future wife, Rebecca, daughter of Rebecca Kingsbury Rice, was born in Wiscasset, in the District of Maine. Rebecca was her mother's namesake—the third daughter to bear the name Rebecca. Rebecca Kingsbury Rice's first namesake died in 1770 of "contagion" at age two. The second Rebecca died immediately after birth in 1773. The third Rebecca survived. She was one of nine children, only five of whom survived infancy. Rebecca's mother, Rebecca Kingsbury Rice, wife of Judge Thomas Rice, loved her surviving Rebecca and was determined to protect her child from harm.

Freeman Parker was five years older than his future wife. He was born in Barnstable on Cape Cod in July 1776, the child of Freeman and Desire Parker. The fact that he was named Freeman in the same month that the thirteen Colonies declared their independence from Britain was a coincidence—Freeman was named for his father, Adjutant Freeman Parker, who was in George Washington's Continental Army at the time his son was born. Adjutant

Freeman Parker died of disease two months later without ever seeing the baby boy who was his namesake.

Rebecca survived the harsh realities of an 18th-century childhood and grew up to marry Freeman. She was "bonny, blithe and gay" and held "a special place in the hearts of all," as her daughter, Ann, told my grandmother in the late 1800s. Rebecca's hair was blond and her brown eyes sparkled. Aunt Ann said that all the good looks came from the Rice side of the family, not the Parker side. Although he was charming, according to Aunt Ann, Freeman Parker's looks were "plain."

Like many New England girls, Rebecca became skilled with a needle and thread and sewed a sampler to prove it. At the bottom of the sampler, below the alphabet and flowering plant, Rebecca stitched,

Rebecca Rice is my Name and with my Needle I Wrought the Same in the Thirteenth year of my age. 1793

Rebecca enjoyed needlework, but it was not enough. She wanted an education, and in 1797, she persuaded her parents to send her to school in Boston. They were pleased that Rebecca wanted to "improve her mind," but Rebecca's vigilant mother was very concerned about her beautiful young daughter being away from home. It was a big step for a 16-year-old, but Rebecca was persistent and off she went to Boston and Miss Druitt's School. Back home in Wiscasset, her family missed her. Her mother sent her butter, cakes, and cheese, and a half-dollar to buy sweet biscuits in case she grew "faint" from studying and needed energy. Her brother Thomas wrote as well. He told Rebecca how much he and their sister Sally missed her and could not wait to see her. "We all send our love to you." Sally was already married to a prosperous timber merchant and living in a splendid Wiscasset house with a tall case clock in her front hall, ticking, chiming, and showing the sun and moon rising and setting over a ship forever at sea.

At first it seemed safe enough at Miss Druitt's School, until Rebecca's letters home revealed that she wanted to use her needle skills to make a dress to wear to parties in Boston. In particular, she talked about mixers with the opposite sex "at Mrs. Langdon's." Rebecca asked for money to make a silk dress. By early June 1797 the alarm bells were ringing loudly in Wiscasset. On June 5, her mother wrote Rebecca, "Be careful of the fine stories that the young gentlemen will tell you at Mrs. Langdon's. Let not the thought of Death be ever out of your mind." Rebecca's mother heard nothing from Rebecca that eased her anxiety and, on June 29, she wrote again: "I would have you take care of young gentlemen; they will tell you a thousand fine stories; you must not put your trust in any. I would not have you go to Mrs. Langdon's much; never stay there in the evening."

During the month of July there were no more letters. Rebecca's mother may have thought that her advice had been heeded but maternal calm did not last. Talk of parties in Boston popped up again. On August 17, Rebecca's mother wrote her, "I would not have you go out at night with a gentleman without some lady" as a chaperone.

Rebecca's mother wheeled in more artillery. Rebecca's brother Thomas, more than 10 years older than Rebecca, wrote to her in August, warning, "Be careful and attentive that you may have no reason to repent."

The anxious letters from Rebecca's mother and older brother did not put an end to it. In September Rebecca's mother decided it was time to bring in Rebecca's father and, on September 4, 1797, Judge Rice wrote Rebecca to put an end to the subject once and for all. Hiding behind his wife, the judge wrote, "Your mother thinks you can do without a gown." Judge Rice urged Rebecca to "polish your manners and improve your mind [rather] than adorn your person in gay cloaths." Like her friend, Eliza Southgate from Scarborough, Rebecca could improve her mind by mastering geometry. Her anxious father concluded, "Your youth and inexperience require you to be constantly watchful. There are many who feel no remorse at the ruin of innocence."

Rebecca returned to Wiscasset in the fall of 1797. There is no evidence that her innocence had been ruined. While in Boston she had received enough money from home to make a silk blouse, if not a "gown." (For some reason, a blouse alone was considered less dangerous than a dress.) There was silk left over from making the blouse and, after returning home from Boston, Rebecca used it to make a gift for her mother: an embroidered scene showing a vase of flowers with a dove of peace hovering above it. To the left of the dove a small bird holds a branch in its beak, as if holding out a gift for the larger dove.

A few years later, on September 2, 1801, when she was 20, Rebecca went with her family to Freeman Parker's ordination as minister of the new Dresden church. One of the speakers at the ordination, Reverend Josiah Winship, admonished Freeman, then 25, "Flee youthful lusts which war against the soul." Reverend Winship's dour admonition against "lusts" was lost on Freeman and Rebecca, if they heard it at all.

In later years their children, the five Parker girls, would say that their parents fell in love at first sight. This may have been what Rebecca and Freeman wanted them to believe, but the story was more complicated.

When Rebecca met Freeman at his 1801 ordination, she was secretly engaged to Moses Porter of Biddeford, Maine. Moses was studying to become a lawyer and announcing the engagement before he could make a living might not be well-received by the older generation. Moses did, however, confide in his cousin, Eliza Southgate. Eliza promised that she would "...keep your attachment a secret, for which I am prepared to receive your thanks." However, the cat started to creep out of the bag and, in October 1801, Eliza told Moses that she had been asked "a dozen times" whether he and Rebecca were engaged. "How such things get about!"

Eliza enthusiastically supported marrying for love, although she expressed her "opinion that not one woman in a hundred marries for love." Although she cattily told Moses that she thought Rebecca's beautiful brown eyes sparkled more than her intellect, she understood his passion. He imagined an idyllic rural life with Rebecca. Eliza understood. She talked about his dreams of romance in the last letter she wrote to him in 1802:

> *Rebecca would do charmingly. I know you are imagining her*
> *the partner of all your joys and cares, of all your harmony and*
> *content with your description of rural happiness. With her you*
> *imagine you could quit the world and almost live happy in a*
> *desert.*

But it was not to be. Moses died of malaria on his way back to Maine from the West Indies in July 1802. Rebecca's subsequent romance with Freeman Parker was surely not the love at first sight that the Parker girls imagined. Rebecca undoubtedly needed time to get over Moses Porter.

Nevertheless, Rebecca and Freeman eventually grew close. Freeman's eyesight was failing and it is unclear if this gave Rebecca pause or ultimately drew her closer to him. But now in her early 20s, she may have felt pressure to marry. Freeman, like her father, had a degree from Harvard. His family background and career were acceptable. He was intelligent and had a cheerful personality.

I do not know if Freeman knew about Moses Porter, but it was a small world and the "attachment" had been a leaky secret. In any event, Freeman was attracted by Rebecca's intelligence, independent spirit, and interest in women's education. He joked with her about it and, in 1803, gave her a book by the English author Hannah More, *Strictures on the Modern System of Female Education*, reprinted in Boston the year before. On the flyleaf of the book Freeman wrote in handwriting made unsteady by his poor eyesight:

Miss Rebecca Rice. Presented to her by an Enemy of the modern system of female education. 1803.

A satirist and abolitionist, Hannah More has been compared to Jonathan Swift. In her book, she skewered the prevailing view among men in England that women and Africans were intellectually inferior to Englishmen. In her 18th-century prose, Hannah More observes at the very outset of her book that "until men and women, and until Africans and Europeans" are given equal access to education, their intellectual abilities "can never be fairly ascertained."

Rebecca took Freeman's inscription on Hannah More's book as the joke it was intended to be.

It is apparent that Freeman and Rebecca did not keep themselves entirely free of the "youthful lusts" mentioned in Reverend Josiah Winship's dour warning at Freeman's ordination in 1801. In the summer of 1804, the Kennebec and Sheepscot Rivers offered the couple cool and shady places along the rivers to escape the heat, talk, read a book together, and grow closer. They were married in November of that same year—a sensible move after moments of summer passion and before a visible pregnancy led to gossip. Their first-born child, little Rebecca, was born on April 22, 1805, just five months after the wedding. Four more healthy Parker girls—Sarah, Ann, Elizabeth, and Peggy—would follow in rapid succession.

Rebecca and Freeman gave little Rebecca the middle name Desire, after Freeman's mother, Desire Parker. It was also an appropriate name for their beautiful and healthy love child conceived months before they were married. Rebecca and Freeman, neither 17th-century Puritans nor Victorian prudes, were children of the Enlightenment—the man of God and his bride with the sparkling eyes were human.

Freeman's eyesight continued to deteriorate. Totally blind by 1807, he was determined not to let it stop him from being a minister. The irony of the name "Freeman" cannot have been lost on him—from 1807 he would be imprisoned by darkness and become known as the Blind Preacher of Dresden.

Before his eyesight failed, Freeman wrote 60 sermons on as many topics for Rebecca to read to him over and over again, as he prepared for future Sundays when he could no longer read. She read aloud sermons, books, articles, and letters that he could no longer read. She wrote the letters he could no longer write to his mother in Barnstable and his friends. In good humor, Rebecca wrote her mother-in-law, Desire Parker, after returning from visiting her in Barnstable. Before reaching Maine, she told her mother-in-law that she and Freeman had spent the night at "a miserable road-house" in Andover, where all night they engaged in "close combat" with bedbugs until Rebecca escaped to a chair, leaving "Mr. P." to continue the good fight alone.

Freeman did not hide his blindness. When he went out of their house in Dresden, he wore blind man's glasses with opaque, violet lenses. People could see he was blind and respectfully made way for him. His glasses folded into a small red leather case and, just as any wife might do, Rebecca helped him find the glasses whenever he mislaid them.

Life was not easy for young couples in early 1800s Dresden and nearby Wiscasset. Thomas Jefferson signed into law the Embargo Act of 1807, imposing a ban on trade between the United States and foreign nations in an attempt to stop impressment of American sailors into the British Navy for the war with Napoleon. The Embargo fell like a hammer on New England, which depended on trade with Britain. Business and jobs were lost. And, before it was much more than a dot on the map, Dresden stopped growing. Wiscasset, too, declined.

As local economic conditions worsened, Freeman Parker made a political blunder. From the pulpit he supported Jefferson's Embargo. His words reflected a sincere political belief but it was an unpopular view in northern New England where the population largely despised Jefferson and was being crushed by the Embargo. Freeman almost lost his job. But perhaps because he was blind, his congregation felt sorry for him and did not fire him. The effects of the Embargo grew worse when war with England was declared in 1812. To avoid the dangers of putting to sea Wiscasset's ships sat idle in the harbor. As economic paralysis hardened, Rebecca's father's health failed. Judge Rice died in 1812 not long before Congress declared war against England.

Dresden never recovered from the economic collapse. I do not know how long Freeman's salary at the church continued at the level of $500 per year but Dresden and Wiscasset became backwaters. In the years that followed the War of 1812, the best and the brightest moved west to places like Detroit. Freeman Parker's congregation dwindled. Because of his blindness, Rebecca took over entries in the record book of the Dresden church but in 1826 the entries stopped altogether. The congregation could no longer fill the church or afford a minister. Freeman was let go.

The Parkers sold their Dresden house. Freeman, Rebecca, and the five girls moved into the cold and drafty house with low ceilings that Judge Rice had bought as a small hovel in Wiscasset in the 1760s. The judge had expanded the hovel, whose owner had been killed in an Indian raid, and developed it into a rambling Cape Cod cottage. Rice, his wife, and their five children lived in the old cottage until they moved into a fine redbrick Federal home next door during the more prosperous years after the Revolution.

By 1826, Judge Rice and his wife were long dead and the red brick house had been sold. With the help of Rebecca and the girls, Freeman was able to eke out a living from a wharf and store he bought in Wiscasset supplemented with stipends from Boston missionary societies. As a minister, he continued to make a few dollars here and there—such as $5 for a funeral sermon, as a guest preacher in Wiscasset and elsewhere—but life in Wiscasset cannot have been easy, or free of stress and marital conflicts.

Rebecca died in 1843. She was 62, although in Freeman's mind's eye she stayed 26—the age she had been when he could still see her. When she died, he acknowledged that in their 40-year marriage he was blessed, though they had had "many severe trials, almost inseparable from" any marriage. Rebecca had been the light of his life and now he knew "full well the meaning of the word *alone.*" With his wife gone he did, no doubt, feel alone, but three of his five daughters still lived with him—Ann, Elizabeth, and Peggy. Ann, in particular, became her father's new eyes.

With Ann's help, Freeman lived on for more than 10 years without Rebecca. After petitioning Congress to vote against the Kansas–Nebraska Act, which enraged him because it permitted the extension of slavery, Freeman Parker died in 1854. He was remembered as a man who could and did speak on any subject, with one exception. He could not and did not speak about his blindness.

Aunt Ann rattled around the ancient house in Wiscasset until she died in 1899. She passed along hundreds of memories, the Blind Preacher's collection of books, stacks of his sermons, a 1799 "oration" by Freeman on the death of George Washington that year, and most precious of all, the 1797 letters to Rebecca while she was at Miss Druitt's in Boston. Aunt Ann also handed down two gold lockets with braided blond hair, untouched by gray. One of the lockets is square, with a black enamel border, the other is oval, nearly round, also gold, but with no black border. The inscription on the back of both reads:

Rebecca Parker
Obt. Nov. 6, 1843
Aged 62 years

Both men and women wore mourning jewelry in the Victorian era and I do not know to whom the lockets belonged. Aunt Ann? Freeman? One of the other Parker girls?

I prefer the oval locket without the black frame. It has a thin gold vine border around the glass above the blond braids, which is reminiscent of the border on the sampler of the girl who later went to Miss Druitt's to improve her mind but who longed to make a silk dress for parties in Boston. She was the young woman who first fell in love with a law student who died of malaria while they were secretly engaged. She was the woman who, two years later, married the Blind Preacher of Dresden. Her eyes became his eyes and she raised their five girls.

The gold oval locket brings to my mind the beautiful young girl with blond hair and sparkling brown eyes. The last two decades of her life must have been a struggle as she and the unemployed Blind Preacher lived on through Wiscasset's steady decline. Her married life with Freeman cannot have been the rural idyll she had imagined with Moses Porter.

Aunt Ann was the last of the Parker girls to live in the old, cold Wiscasset home. A nephew, who had prospered in Chicago, sent her a check for $25. In the accompanying letter he explained how Aunt Ann could go to the bank in Wiscasset and cash it. No doubt the money helped her make ends meet in the home where she now lived alone with Freeman's and Rebecca's possessions, including the witchcraft judge's books.

CHAPTER 4.

The Art Student
(1860–1936)

My father taught me to be "a cheerful loser,"
and to "keep a stiff upper lip," and to carry on
under all difficulties.

Isabel Erskine Brewster, 1934

I︎T WAS my grandmother, Isabel Erskine Brewster, who inherited the witchcraft judge's books along with other books and family papers from Aunt Ann. I do not know if Grandmother Brewster ever looked at Freeman Parker's book collection or Stoughton's eerie notes. Grandmother Brewster was interested in other things. She was an art student and played the banjo. But, after the death in 1899 of her Aunt Ann, the last of the Parker girls, she inherited everything that remained in the Wiscasset house. Grandmother Brewster died in 1936, five years before I was born.

Aunt Ann lived out the end of her life alone in the old house in Wiscasset. She was Grandmother Brewster's favorite aunt— in fact, her great-aunt. The players of different ages and generations are confusing so let me take you on a short and, I hope, not too exhausting genealogical journey. Aunt Ann was the younger sister of the love child, Rebecca Desire Parker, who was born in 1805.

According to Aunt Ann, her sister Rebecca Desire Parker got all the good looks from the Rice side of the family and there were none left for the rest of the Parker girls. Thus, the younger four sisters inherited plain looks from the Parker side of the family. The good-looking one, Rebecca Desire Parker, married Colonel John Erskine and was Grandmother Brewster's grandmother.

As a little girl, Grandmother Brewster visited Aunt Ann in Wiscasset and Aunt Ann told her wonderful stories of the past and about the furniture in the ancient rambling cottage. "Judge Rice worked at his desk in this round-backed chair," she would say. Or "That tilt-top tea table belonged to Freeman Parker's mother, Desire Parker," and "The grandfather's clock was Aunt Sally's clock," referring to the Parker girls' Aunt Sally, who, along with her brother, mother, and father, worried about her adventurous little sister Rebecca when she was a 16-year-old at school in Boston in 1797.

Grandmother Brewster's eyes opened wide as she learned about family things dating back to the 18th century. Aunt Ann also told her about the regal origins of the Erskines in Scotland. "We have royal blood in our veins." Grandmother Brewster's eyes opened wider. When it came to the family possessions, Aunt Ann's statements were well sourced. After all, Ann's mother, Rebecca, the Blind Preacher's wife, knew first-hand about furniture like the round-backed chair, the tilt-top table, and Aunt Sally's clock. But the statement about royal blood was far from the truth—the Erskines who made it from Scotland to Wiscasset were the poorest members of that Scottish clan. Grandmother Brewster was not above gilding the lily.

Grandmother Brewster's father, Robert Parks, taught her to be a "cheerful loser" and to carry on "under all difficulties." He was a grain-and-commodities broker in Chicago and, later, New York, where the family moved in 1866 when Grandmother Brewster was six. They lived in a hotel on Madison Square. Grandmother Brewster went to school, first on lower Fifth Avenue and later to

Miss Haines School at 10 Gramercy Park South. By then, Grandmother Brewster was 12 and walked to school down Broadway to 19th Street. She always stopped at the corner of 19th Street to look through the high wrought-iron fence around the Goelet estate, an anomaly in Manhattan even then. The Goelet mansion stood in the center of a large lawn. Pausing by the fence the 12-year-old Isabel could glimpse cows, peacocks, pheasants, and guinea hens. Of equal interest to a young schoolgirl, next door to the mansion was Pursell's Bakery where they sold chocolate éclairs.

The family was neither rich nor poor. Isabel's father rarely took a vacation. "When I have had the money I have not had the time, and when I had the time I did not have the money." He did have time and money for music, horse races, horses, and his only child, Isabel. Robert Parks loved opera and music of all kinds. At home he sang Stephen Foster songs to Isabel. In turn she took up the banjo and never put it down.

Grandmother Brewster loved music, but her mother inspired her to paint and she became even more passionate about art. She studied with several American and European artists, even selling a few paintings. The sales "gave her the courage and ambition to continue painting." Long after she grew up, she continued her art student's life in New York.

In the late 1880s she met Samuel Dwight Brewster, whom she called Dwight. They enjoyed each other. They courted in Manhattan and during the summer horse racing season in Saratoga. More than once Dwight asked her to marry him, but she liked her art student's life and put off his proposals. He broke off the relationship.

They did not see each other for five years—a time that was painful for Isabel—but they met again by chance in the early 1890s, when she interrupted her Bohemian days to have dinner with her parents at Delmonico's on Beaver and William Street.

Dwight was at another table but stopped to talk with Isabel and her parents. She had never seen him "so handsome and attractive." She regretted turning down his marriage proposals. As he left the table to rejoin his friends, Isabel, a less-than-bashful Bohemian said, "Come and see me." She followed up with a card and he did.

They were married at St. Thomas Church on Fifth Avenue on April 19, 1893. She was 33, he was 42. By the time of their marriage, Dwight had become a partner of a textile-manufacturing firm, Deering Milliken, and had started on his journey to wealth. They bought and moved into a beautiful brownstone at 126 West 80th Street between Columbus and Amsterdam, where both Uncle Sydney and Pop were born—Sydney in 1897, Pop in 1901. The textile business, Dwight, and Isabel Brewster all prospered. While Pop was still in a crib, the family moved to a more fashionable neighborhood, buying a townhouse off Fifth Avenue at 45 West 49th Street, long since leveled to make way for 30 Rockefeller Plaza.

My grandmother's parents, Isabel and Robert Parks, had died one after the other within a year of Isabel's and Dwight's wedding. They were both in their 50s. It was no longer the 18th century, but life could still end suddenly and unexpectedly. Grandmother Brewster continued to play the banjo, but following her mother's death she would never again pick up a paintbrush. Instead, she said, her creative and artistic ability "found expression in my home."

Artistic expression of this kind started in earnest with the townhouse off Fifth Avenue. As Dwight made more money in the textile business, my grandmother spent lavishly on the townhouse. She had it "painted and re-decorated from attic to cellar." When Sydney was nearly 10 years old, and Pop was little more than a toddler, disaster struck the newly renovated townhouse. Celebrating the completion of the work, Isabel and Dwight invited friends for drinks and then went to the theater, leaving Sydney and Pop with the nanny. While they were at the theater, oily rags left by the painters caught fire in a closet at the top of the stairs near the nursery. The fire spread rapidly and soon the stairway caught fire. It was still early. Sydney had not yet gone to bed. The nanny smelled smoke and rushed to the nursery. She picked up Pop, asleep in his bed, rolled him in a blanket and ran down the burning staircase. Sydney slid down the bannister. News of the fire reached my grandparents at the theater and they rushed home. The top two floors were destroyed by the fire and the rest of the house was destroyed by water from the fire hoses. Grandmother Brewster kept the "stiff upper lip" and "cheerful" response to loss that her father had taught her. The house was in ruins, but the boys were safe. Once more she indulged her artistic talents—they redid the house and lived there for nearly two more decades.

Grandfather Brewster continued to prosper and Grandmother Brewster needed more room to express her creativity. Soon after buying the townhouse off Fifth Avenue, they bought the Big House in Glen Cove as a summer home—its 35 rooms were crying out for the talents of the former art student.

Brushes with death continued to follow Sydney. When he was 15 and Pop was 11, there was a flu outbreak at St. Paul's School in Concord, New Hampshire. The school shut down and Sydney came home to escape the epidemic. But there was no safe haven on 49th Street. Antibiotics were decades away and Sydney contracted a mastoid infection. His life hung by a thread for months. At one point, the doctors told my grandmother that there was no hope, she and my grandfather must prepare for the worst. Sydney survived.

After Sydney recovered, life was good again. My grandmother kept buying things for their homes and playing her banjo. The

Brewster family made a grand tour of Europe by carriage. The banjo came with them on the grand tour.

Years later, as the guns of August boomed in Europe in 1914, Sydney went on to Princeton. But death soon stalked him again. In 1917 he switched his major to the new field of "aeronautical studies" hoping to join the war effort as a fighter pilot, as soon as the United States entered the fight. He went to Foggia, Italy, for his initial flight training and then to England and France for more training. He was positioned close to the front when his squadron went into action. The life expectancy for a pilot in the First World War was not long. Planes like the one Sydney flew were nicknamed "flying coffins." Again, my grandparents prepared for the worst.

Sydney was shot down in a dogfight over northern France. With his engine knocked out, his gunner, Jones, kept firing at the pursuing German plane. The German plane went down in flames and Sydney glided into a field. He and Jones walked away and hitched a ride to Verdun in a farmer's truck. Sydney had cheated death again. He came home and, after graduating from Princeton, married his Manhattan sweetheart, Tracy Lyon.

For Grandmother Brewster, painful losses followed. Dwight grew in both wealth and girth. With every passing year, his wealth increased and so did his weight. He looked more and more like William Howard Taft and less and less like the handsome 40-year-old who had moved the art student to say, "Come and see me." His health was suffering. The celebration of Sydney's safe return from war was cut short—Dwight died, unexpectedly, just after the Armistice. My grandmother's grief was nearly "insupportable."

Grief followed grief. Just a few years later, Sydney died. Grandmother Brewster could not speak of the horror of her son's death and, instead, resorted to saying only that he "went West." The unspeakable reality was that Sydney died in a murder-suicide in 1926, first killing his wife, Tracy, and then himself. It was a dark family secret that Sam and I overheard decades later through our bedroom door.

Sydney and Tracy lived in Glen Head, a village a few miles inland from Glen Cove. In their home Sydney found a love letter from another man to Tracy. There was a violent argument followed by gunshots. A servant found their bodies on the bedroom floor. Sydney's was near the door, while Tracy lay dead several feet away with her left leg folded under her right and the pistol a few inches from her right foot. Nassau County District Attorney Woods found no reason to conduct a Grand Jury investigation. There was no sign of a break-in and the crime scene revealed no evidence pointing to the involvement of anyone other than Sydney and Tracy. In the District Attorney's plausible view, Sydney murdered Tracy and then killed himself after discovering the love letter. There was motive and the pistol belonged to Sydney.

Sydney's horrifying death nearly crushed Grandmother Brewster. It was also devastating for Pop. It was the greatest test of my great-grandfather's lesson that his daughter should take losses "cheerfully" and "carry on under all difficulties." Grandmother Brewster "was given strength to help" Pop carry on after losing his brother. And, in the end, helping him helped her.

Channeling more of her creative talent into her homes also helped Grandmother Brewster survive. She moved from the townhouse on 49th Street to a 20-room duplex apartment at 800 Park Avenue. She saw the move as "a great diversion to reassemble all my treasures, which seemed to form themselves into pictures in the new groupings."

Grandmother Brewster expressed herself still further by remodeling her summer home, the Big House in Glen Cove. When she and my grandfather bought it at the beginning of the century, it was a rambling, brown-shingled, beach "cottage" with a roof over the driveway at the front door. Carriages could pull up to the front of the house and their passengers, protected from the weather, could alight onto the front steps of the house. It was called a *porte-cochère*. Frederick, my grandparents' coachman, would stop their carriage beneath the porte-cochère so that they could get in and out of it when they were at the Big House for the summer; to unload at the beginning of the summer when my grandparents first arrived from the City; and to reload as they prepared to return to the City at the end of the summer. For local jaunts without luggage when they did not need the carriage, my grandfather kept a flashy two-seater in the stable, which he drove with the carriage horses in tandem.

My grandmother saw the rambling brown-shingled Glen Cove beach cottage with its porte-cochère just as she saw all of life—not as it was but as she wanted it to be: a Greek Revival mansion. That would be a better setting for Aunt Sally's clock and the other 18th-century treasures she had inherited from the house in Wiscasset. She transformed the house into her vision. A high Greek Revival pediment supported by four tall Doric columns replaced the porte-cochère. Doric columns were also placed around the shady porch on the west end of the Big House, where you could sip iced tea on a hot summer afternoon. The brown shingles vanished and the entire house was painted white.

In a breathtaking transformation the artist-magician in my grandmother had changed the beach "cottage" into a version of Mount Vernon or the White House. Both the Big House and the sprawling apartment at 800 Park Avenue were re-fitted with 18th-century details. Grandmother Brewster could move her treasures back and forth, if she chose, to "form themselves into pictures in the new groupings" in either home. She did just that. Sometimes Judge Rice's blockfront desk and Aunt Sally's clock were at 800 Park and sometimes in Glen Cove. If Aunt Sally's clock was in Glen Cove and the art student wanted to hear the chimes or watch the time on it, she had the "clock man" from Tiffany's come out to wind it.

Later in life, Mom encouraged Grandmother Brewster to write down what Aunt Ann had told her about her family's history in Wiscasset. She took the bait and wrote a 300-page vanity book entitled *Recollections*. Nor did she stop with Aunt Ann's observations such as which chair Judge Rice sat in; rather, she created an entire world, not necessarily as it was, but as she chose it to be. She wrote glorified histories of the Parker, Rice, Erskine, Parks, and Brewster families. The Erskines were exalted as Scottish lords, not the illiterate poor members of a Scottish clan who fled to the American colonies. Her book includes an engraving of a supposed ancestor—a Norman knight who accompanied William the Conqueror to England in 1066.

Both family history and her own recollections were carefully edited. Painful details were banished. Sydney's heroism as a fighter pilot was described in detail, but his death was barely mentioned. Grandmother Brewster's recollections were, at least in part, more re-creations than recollections. She had 50 copies of *Recollections* printed for family and friends. She died two years later, in 1936.

Grandmother Brewster's creative re-writing of history, like her re-arranging of the treasures in her homes, was a "great diversion" that allowed her to survive the hammer blows of life, including the horrific death of her beloved child who had survived so much from the moment he slid down the bannister on a burning staircase to the time he walked away from his fighter plane when it hit the ground in northern France.

Mom and my sister, Isabel, my grandmother's namesake, said that Grandmother Brewster was a warm and sentimental person, that she was a big hugger. Two of the paintings she did as an art student before her parents' death hung in the Big House and reflected her warmth and vision of life. One was a long horizontal painting of flowers. Roses? Peonies? A combination? I don't remember for sure, but it hung over the sleigh bed in the master bedroom, as if to proclaim, "I don't care what they say. By force of will and imagination, I will make my life a bed of roses." The second was of the path leading to the front door of the ancient family home in Wiscasset. Bushes flower along the path and warm sunlight falls upon the scene. Nothing in the painting suggests the cold interior described by my father's cousin Woolcott, who grew up in the house. Woolcott told me that in the winter your hair was apt to freeze when you got out of the bathtub.

The art student dealt with the harsh realities of life by becoming the dreamer in the Stephen Foster song her father sang to her when she sat on his knee in the 1860s:

Beautiful dreamer,
Wake unto me
Starlight and dewdrops
Are awaiting thee.
Sounds of the rude world
Heard in the day
Led by the moonlight
Have all passed away.

As far as I know, Grandmother Brewster never stopped playing the banjo. After she died, no one had the heart to take it off the lid of the grand piano in Glen Cove. It lay there on the piano in the big room in the Big House until 1993, when the Greek Revival fantasy that the beautiful dreamer had created was sold.

CHAPTER 5.

War Babies
(1939–1945)

Many there are, who, having been born to
fair Estates have quite undone themselves by
marriage...

The Worth Of A Penny, *p. 12*
Henry Peacham, 1641

S AM AND I were both born a few years after Grandmother Brewster died. Technically, we were pre-war babies, since Sam was born in 1939 and I was born in 1941 three weeks before Pearl Harbor, but the world we entered was at war. Mom came home with me from the hospital the day Pearl Harbor was bombed, following a difficult Caesarian section, which kept her in the hospital for several weeks after my birth. With the country suddenly at war, things like my baptism were put on hold for years; all the adults in the family had other things to do. Mom became a nurse's aide and Pop joined the Coast Guard. Gramps, General Thomas Darrah, Mom's father, who had retired from his army career before the war, came out of retirement to help run civilian defense in New York State.

Pop was generally away from home on a ship patrolling the coast for German submarines. One night he came home with a fired artillery shell and gave it to Sam and me after we rushed to the front door to hug him. That awesome shell stood nearly 2ft tall and several inches in diameter. Sniffing the opening at the top of the shell, Sam and I could still smell the burnt gunpowder. We were more familiar with the very small shells Alfred ejected from his .22 rifle as we followed him around to watch him shoot squirrels out of the trees. Alfred Waltz, the teenage son of our German gardener, Joe Waltz, lived in the East Cottage with Joe and Mrs. Waltz. Sam and I liked following him on his squirrel hunts. His father's accent was interesting but Joe Waltz turned out to be an anti-Semite and Nazi sympathizer. While Pop was patrolling the coast looking for German submarines, Joe Waltz told Sam and me that we should march up and down the back driveway in front of the East Cottage, chanting, "The Jews killed Christ."

There was a fear of wartime food shortages so Joe raised vegetables for us across from the cottages on an acre of open land in front of Mom's greenhouse. The vegetable garden was separated from the back drive by a long grape arbor. On the far side of the garden, near the front drive, there was a path that led from the Big House to the greenhouse and was bordered on either side by a row of peony bushes. Beyond the path were planted asparagus and raspberry patches and a long hedge that screened all the food-growing areas and the greenhouse from the front drive.

Mom's "old hens with a new look" went into a monster wood-paneled walk-in freezer in the kitchen, while tomatoes and other vegetables ended up in mason jars in the cold-pantry next to the shaded back porch behind the kitchen and maids' dining room. With the Concord grapes from the arbor, Mom made grape juice and grape jelly, which ended up in the pantry refrigerator until Sam and I consumed them.

Throughout the war we had sheep and ducks on the lawn below the terrace. The sheep had something against boys and regularly butted Sam and me, but I became special friends with one of the ducks until I opened the kitchen refrigerator door one day and found my friend, not yet plucked, lying dead on his back. The kitchen refrigerator, which we called the icebox, had recently replaced a real icebox. The ice man continued to deliver blocks of ice to the back door and we went on using the icebox long after we had the walk-in freezer and pantry refrigerator, because the ice man needed the money. Pop couldn't tell him we no longer had any use for block ice.

Joe Waltz eventually went to work for another family and Peter Renaldo, who had a young family and looked like a movie star, became our gardener. Peter, Mrs. Renaldo, little Peter, Bobby, and Mary Ann moved into the East Cottage.

I don't know whether it was one of the Renaldos or the garbage man, but one Christmas Eve someone left a kitten under the back porch of the Big House. Stacks of firewood and a shed for the garbage pails lined the walls under the porch and Sam and I found the kitten huddled next to the wood piles away from the snow that had blown through the latticework. Mom's friend, John Harges, had a mink farm in New Jersey and bred miniature, short-legged French poodles. He had given us two of his poodles, Domino and Miss Julie, but we did not have a cat.

Sam and I thought Pop did not like cats because he had killed tigers. We offered to give up our allowances if Pop would let us keep the kitten. We knew that Mom loved animals. With her encouragement and Pop's agreement we kept the kitten without losing any allowance. The kitten was female and Mom named her Winnie Winkle after a comic book heroine who worked to support her parents and adopted brother, reflecting the changing role of women. Winnie was a very smart cat. Cats are carnivores, but I swear that Winnie learned to hold and nibble a piece of buttery corn on the cob between her front paws. Within a year she had produced eight kittens in the flower pantry. Mom and Pop let us keep one, but the rest were given away, and Winnie was "fixed."

Sam and I continued our exploration of our kingdom. The basement of the house was as interesting as the attic. Just inside the rear entrance, under the back porch and garbage pails, was a utility room on the right with the compressor for the walk-in freezer in the kitchen above. Next to the compressor was a door to Peter Renaldo's tool closet. At the far end of the utility room, past Peter's workbench, was a wine cellar, which still had some bottles of Madeira from before the First World War. Across the hall from the utility room was a laundry room with a hotel-scale mangle, which Mrs. O'Brien or Mrs. Gabrish used to press the sheets. Mrs. O'Brien and Mrs. Gabrish did the laundry in huge sinks, washing and rinsing the sheets and then running them through the long rollers of the mangle. They ironed clothing on an ironing board. There was a small coal-fired Franklin stove at one end of the laundry while farther into the basement was the boiler room with stalls filled with coal. At the far end of the basement, beneath the big room, was a crawl space filled with cobwebs. It was there, in that dark crawl space, that I was sure the Evil Spirits lived having escaped from the flyleaf of the witchcraft judge's book when Sam and I opened the steamer trunk in the big attic. I was afraid to go in the crawl space for fear of meeting the specters that haunted Peacham as he lay moaning on the rack.

Sam and I explored every inch of the house. Sometimes we made a lot of noise and sometimes we were silent as we crept around or played in our room. We overheard things we were not meant to hear, like conversations between Mrs. Hagstrom and Mrs. Swenson, who came in during the week to clean and make the beds. Sam and I loved Mrs. Hagstrom and Mrs. Swenson. They made Christmas cookies and long braided loaves of Swedish coffee bread that I will never forget. I don't remember how often, but we were sometimes sent to stay overnight with Mrs. Hagstrom or Mrs. Swenson, who lived with their families in nearby Red Spring Colony. Our overnights to Red Spring may have been connected to Mom taking Pop to the hospital.

When Sam and I were playing very quietly in our bedroom one morning, we heard Mrs. Hagstrom and Mrs. Swenson talking in low voices in the green room about a magazine article. The green room was a guest room next to our bedroom. The article was about Pop's brother, Sydney. Sam and I knew about Sydney, but only that he was a war hero, a 20-year-old pilot in the United States Expeditionary Force in 1917 and 1918. We knew that in an aerial battle one of the wheels of his plane was shot off, but he still managed to land safely. We also knew about the dogfight in which a German fighter knocked out Sydney's engine, and how Sydney and his gunner, Jones, came down in a field, removed the plane's instruments and cut off the plane's identifying insignia, Number 3. In one of the trunks in the big attic Sam and I had found the "No. 3" insignia, painted on a piece of cloth. In the same trunk, next to the insignia, were Sydney's uniform and a certificate from the Aero Club d'Italia. But Pop never talked with us about Sydney.

The overheard conversation between Mrs. Hagstrom and Mrs. Swenson filled in "the rest of the story." It was a phrase that Sam and I often heard coming in a rich baritone from the radio on the library shelves, when Pop turned it on to listen to Paul Harvey. Harvey commented on the day's news and always ended with the tag line "…and that's the rest of the story." In the whispers that Sam and I heard, we began to learn what we had never been told—a dark truth that had been tucked away like Sydney's uniform in a steamer trunk in the big attic.

We did not learn all the details at that time, but the dark secret was a heavy burden and I made deep connections between the witchcraft books and my family. The take-away was that my family had bad blood. The evil spirits from the spooky books haunted us.

When Sydney and Tracy died in 1926, Pop and Grandmother Brewster went to Woodlawn Cemetery alone and quietly saw Sydney and Tracy buried next to each other in the Brewster family plot. Sydney's and Tracy's names and dates are chiseled on the monument beneath the names of other buried relatives. The scene is peaceful. It was as if Pop and Grandmother Brewster tried to make everything right between the star-crossed lovers.

CHAPTER 6.

The Beach
(c. 1949)

Now money is the World's God, and the Card
which the Devil turns up trump to win the set.
The Worth Of A Penny, *p. 18*

CRESCENT BEACH ROAD, where Sam and I grew up, ends at a public beach, known as Crescent Beach. When Sam and I were little, big kids with their girlfriends sometimes drove souped-up hot rods down Crescent Beach Road at high speed to the public beach and back. Little kids, like Sam and me, were not allowed to walk on Crescent Beach Road because of those speeding cars. It was safer, and also more direct, for us to walk to our private beach by going down the narrow, rutted road behind the Big House called Smuggler's Lane. Because of the ruts, the very occasional car that went that way could not go more than a few miles an hour. Smuggler's Lane went down the hill to a triangle intersection on the flats above the beach. There, another narrow lane went to the right, back up towards Crescent Beach Road and the driveway to the Loenings' house.

At the triangle Smuggler's Lane joined a slightly wider road in the flats and went on to our private beach about a quarter mile farther on. I remember once, during a hurricane, the storm surge swept debris and a rowboat all the way to the triangle. Sam and

I found the battered rowboat incongruously parked hundreds of yards above the high-water mark. Usually the tides at Crescent Beach rise more uneventfully—between 6 and 10 feet depending on the earth's rotation, the lunar cycle. With equal inevitability, memories of childhood rise and fall, and occasionally surge with the emotional tides within us.

The beach played a big part in my earliest years. Long before Sam and I found William Stoughton's books, even before we had bicycles, we would walk down Smuggler's Lane to the private beach that we shared with a few neighbors and which adjoined the public beach at the bottom of Crescent Beach Road. As small boys we spent most of our time in the summer at the beach. Often walking barefoot on the sand, beach pebbles, lanes, and driveway, our small feet became tough as tank treads, impervious to anything except splinters in the dock or a sharp piece of glass. I don't remember any sharp glass on the beach—it may have been carefully picked up or raked up on our well-tended private beach—the only glass we found was collectible, different colored, clear or frosted pieces whose edges had been smoothed by the relentless tides that ground and polished them against the sand.

The Big House was one of eight homes in the North Country Colony, a homeowners' association, which owned both Crescent Beach and the network of private roads and lanes within the Colony. These lanes connected the homes to the public road, via gates, and to the Colony's private beach. The only purpose of the lane that went back up towards Crescent Beach Road from the triangle was to get to the Loenings' place. After Rudolph Loening bought his own beach, beach house, and dock next to our beach, he stopped paying dues to the Colony and the gate connecting his driveway to the Colony lane was locked.

When the Colony was formed in the late 1800s, the residents gave the beach at the end of Crescent Beach Road to the City of Glen Cove as a public beach. Glorified as "Crescent Beach," it was a small rocky sliver of shore next to a barnacle-covered breakwater. Between that beach and our beach, a small stream from Mrs. Luckenbach's pond emptied into the Sound and offered some good clamming for steamer clams below the high-tide mark.

The Colony employed a "beach man." One of his jobs was to keep the public from leaving their miserable patch of public beach and trespassing onto the private beach. This undoubtedly was resented by public beachgoers, including the hot-rodders and their girlfriends, who not only were confined to the very inferior public beach but also had a view of the hundreds of yards of private beach that were enjoyed by a small handful of wealthy families. The public could not even cross the Colony's beach between the high- and low-water marks because unusual Colonial land grants had conveyed the beach to the Colony's predecessors with private land ownership extending below the low-water mark out into the waters of Long Island Sound for a considerable distance. In plain view of the excluded bathers, our private beach afforded the members of the Colony with as fine a sandy beach as you could find on the North Shore of Long Island.

About a hundred yards from the public beach, the Colony had a beach house and a dock, beyond which the beach continued for another hundred yards or more. The dock had two stairways going down into the water and at the far end of the dock a gangway went down to a deep-water float with a canvas-covered deck, diving board, and sturdy swimming ladders for swimmers to climb back up from the water onto the float. The long stretch of beach to the east of the dock was for Colony families and guests. The equally long stretch of beach to the west was the "maids' beach"—used exclusively by the people who worked for the Colony families including, back in the day, the eight mostly Irish maids, butler, coachman (or eventual chauffeur), and gardener who worked for my grandparents.

At the top of the beach, just east of the dock, was the beach house, with a roofed-over flagstone terrace. It had a central hall for parties, with dressing rooms on either side. There were lockers and a solarium—men and boys on one side, women and girls on the other. All of this offered myriad options for the Colony members and their families to swim off the beach or dock, sunbathe on the beach, lie nude on the benches in the single-sex solariums, or sit in the shade on the terrace, as Omy and Gramps often did when they walked down to the beach.

Growing up, I felt guilty about the invidious comparison between our expansive private domain and the miserable patch of public beach. Indeed, I always felt some guilt and a good deal of ambivalence about the things that Grandfather Brewster's money bought. At a deep emotional level, I irrationally associated Gramps's health, success, and strength with his penniless life as a soldier, and I just as irrationally associated Pop's depression, tics, and shakes—as well as Sydney's murder-suicide—with Grandfather Brewster's riches. There was no logic to this, but for much of my life, at some level, more sub-conscious than conscious, I saw wealth and money as evil, a card the Devil played, somehow connected to the "Evil Spirits" of the witchcraft judge's book.

But, before my life experiences gave me these attitudes and feelings and for years before Sam and I discovered Stoughton's books, we spent time at the Colony beach. Then it was a magical place for us. I learned to swim as soon as I learned to walk. As we grew older, we swam longer and longer distances, until eventually we were swimming back and forth between our dock and Rudolph Loening's dock more than a hundred yards to the west. When we were older, we caught immature bluefish, called "snappers" or "baby blues," off the float, or we just sat there with our feet dangling over the edge. One day, I saw a porpoise coming toward the float, surfacing and diving above and below the surface of the water. It came ever closer until, finally, it popped up and rubbed the bottom of my feet with its fin. Yowzer! I jerked my feet up and rolled my body back onto the canvas deck of the float.

Behind the beach was a swamp that extended almost back to the triangle at the bottom of Smuggler's Lane and from the Colony's beach house to Mr. Loening's beach house, which stood at the landward end of a dilapidated dock. The Loenings had a caretaker, who stayed in their beach house in the summer, but Mrs. Loening was an invalid and I do not remember ever seeing either of them at their beach. Sam and I would spend hours exploring the swamp. It was crisscrossed by narrow creeks, which we would jump across. The creeks were home to turtles and skittering fiddler crabs, while the swamp around them had pheasants, rabbits, field mice, and frogs. We brought field mice home to keep as pets in old birdcages that we found in the attic. But Mom would not let us bring them into the house so we kept them outside on the back porch behind the kitchen. We tried to make the mice comfortable by making cotton beds for them and giving them food, but they didn't live long.

A big part of the magic of the beach was Olaf. Olaf was a janitor at the Glen Cove High School and in the summer he was the North Country Colony beach man. He lived on Landing Road with his wife and a Chihuahua. Olaf raked our beach to keep it free from seaweed and flotsam and jetsam. He helped to keep the dock, gangplank, and float in good repair and chased away trespassers from the public beach. Olaf was Norwegian. Swedes, like the Hagstroms, Swensons, and Goransons, outnumbered Norwegians in Glen Cove and so, in self-defense, Olaf liked to sing a song about a "Thousand Swedes running through the weeds, chased by one Norwegian..." Every "w" was pronounced as a "v."

Olaf helped Sam and me find nuggets of "fool's gold," iron pyrite, on the beach. He also told us that whales threw up lumps of something called *ambergris*, which was very valuable and was used to make perfume. He described what it looked like and told us to keep our eyes out for it. We never stopped looking, hoping to make a fortune on whale barf, but, of course, we never found any. Olaf also acted as lifeguard when people were swimming off the beach, dock, and float—he rowed the Colony's rowboat and positioned it near to small children or elderly swimmers, like old Mrs. Nichols and Mrs. Murray, who swam around in circles discussing recipes. I was once told how Olaf had fended off a huge snapping turtle that had escaped from Mrs. Luckenbach's pond and gone into the saltwater. Everyone said that Olaf clobbered the huge turtle with an oar and the infuriated snapping turtle bit a piece of wood out of the oar's blade.

Everyone in the Colony trusted Olaf—parents and very small children alike. Before he retired, when I was perhaps seven, Sam and I spent the night in the beach house with him. In the morning he cooked bacon and eggs for us in a pan over a can of flaming Sterno.

I don't remember what year it was, except that it was the year that friends of Omy and Gramps loaned them a cottage for the summer in Bellport, a beautiful village on the South Shore on the Atlantic Ocean side of Long Island. They spent the summer there instead of in their room on the second floor of the Big House. Their room had a door opening onto a columned second-floor porch that overlooked our terrace and had a view across the Ottleys' long field next door to Long Island Sound over the trees in the distance. The absence of my grandparents cast a dark cloud over our summer, lightened only when Sam and I succeeded in persuading Mom to move our beds onto the porch off Omy and Gramps's room, so that we could sleep outside.

Olaf had retired after the previous summer. No one in the Colony was happy about it. Sam and I were certainly sad. Olaf was replaced as the Colony's beach man by Bill, a caretaker who had been living in the Loenings' beach house. For everyone in the Colony, Olaf had been synonymous with trust. Bill was the successor in that position of trust. Bill had a truck, and one day when Sam was doing something else, Bill asked me if I would like to go for a ride. He said he had to pick up something from his winter apartment near Landing Road. Sam was down the beach doing something else important like poking with his toes below the high-tide mark looking for steamer clams near the creek that came from Mrs. Luckenbach's pond.

I liked the idea of a drive in Bill's truck and we drove to his apartment near Landing Road. Inside, he showed me drawings and photographs of naked girls. I do not remember if I told Sam about the pictures.

Later that same summer, Bill asked me to come into the Loenings' beach house with him. Again he picked a time when Sam was doing something else. My memories of all of this are broken fragments. I remember there was a lot of poison ivy around the Loenings' beach house and I recall Bill saying that poison ivy did not bother him, that he could rub his hands in it and not get a rash—to prove his point, he did just that. Inside the beach cottage, Bill said he wanted to show me something I could do with girls when I got older. I remember him taking off my bathing suit and touching me. He took his bathing suit off. There is much I don't remember…the parts of the experience that I do remember are unspeakable.

When I got back to our beach, I told Sam in graphic detail about the things that Bill had done. My brother said, "Whatever you do, don't tell anybody." I think he added, "especially Mom and Pop." I do not know whether Sam said that because what had happened was too shameful to reveal to anyone, or because he was afraid that he might get in trouble for not protecting me.

I followed Sam's instructions and did not tell a soul. But I quickly developed a terrible case of poison ivy in the very private places where Bill had touched me, possibly intentionally and sadistically. I told Mom that I had poison ivy and that it hurt. When I showed her the painful swelling she said, "How did you get poison ivy there?"

Sticking to Sam's instructions, I lied, and made up a story.

I told no one what happened until the end of the summer when my older brother, Tom, and sister, Isabel, came home from wherever they had been in July and August. Isabel cornered me. She wanted to know everything that her baby brother had been doing while she was away. "I want all the details," she said. She would not take no for an answer. I blurted out the whole thing, all the gory details about Bill in the Loenings' beach house.

I know that Isabel told Mom and that there were urgent conversations about contacting the police and lawyers. I was not part of the conversations. I overheard parts of some of them, but other than my disclosures to Sam and Isabel, I do not remember anyone talking with me about the incident—not the police, not a doctor, not Mom, not Pop.

My memories of that day in the Loenings' beach cottage stir powerful emotions. Even now, roughly 70 years later, I feel vulnerable, hurt, unprotected, filled with anxiety and rage. Bill left me with permanent scars and emotional pain. But I believe such stories must be told, they should not be swept under the rug. Harm and rage that will not go away, no matter how many decades pass, need to be voiced and heard.

I do not know whether Omy and Gramps found out what happened. I do know that Mom spoke with Omy on the phone every day without fail and that if she told Omy about the incident then Omy told Gramps. It was around that time that Gramps made a scrapbook for me. He was a wonderful sketch artist and on the book's first page he did a very fine pen-and-ink drawing of the head and shoulders and huge front paws of a male lion. The lion was *couchant* with a regal mane. Above it, in fine calligraphy, Gramps penned, in capital letters

RICHARD THE LIONHEARTED
HIS SCRAPBOOK

Over the many decades since I left the nest on Crescent Beach Road, I have had personal and professional failures and defeats. I am grateful that I have also had more than my fair share of successes and victories, perhaps "big frog, small pond" successes and victories, but they are still very sweet for me. Despite, and through, the ups and downs life goes on. As Churchill reminded us, the only thing that really matters is the ability to get up when you are knocked down and get on with it. "Success is not final, failure is not fatal; it is the courage to continue that counts." I never heard Gramps speak those words, but that is what he showed me.

I never knew Gramps as a soldier. My relationship with him was personal, a family relationship, but I knew his story: After his mother died, Gramps's father abandoned him and his sister and brother. That abandonment, coming so close on the heels of his mother's death, must have been a very hard fall. But he picked himself up, dusted himself off, and got on with it.

Whenever I am kicked in the pants or in the teeth, I remember Gramps—the soldier who won Silver Stars for courage in battles on beaches and in jungles over a hundred years ago and who gave me the courage to continue and the guts to tell the story.

CHAPTER 7.

Life on the Gold Coast

(1950s and '60s)

A fool and his money are soon parted.
My grandfather, Samuel Dwight Brewster,
on seeing Pop's motor vehicle, c. 1915

LIKE SYDNEY, the Pop that I loved and did not see enough owned
a pistol. After the war, when Pop was in the hospital following his
stroke, Sam and I climbed up on a chair to investigate the top
drawers of Pop's bureau. We found a revolver and bullets. The evil
spirits from the witchcraft judge's books may have been connected
with whatever bad blood led to Sydney's murder-suicide, but luckily they did not make Sam and me do anything stupid with Pop's
gun. For the first of many times, the evil spirits looked the other
way.

Pop and Sydney had other things in common. Pop was also a
pilot and kept a single engine plane at an airfield in Hempstead
when I was little. A 1949 Piper Cub, it was several generations
of aeronautical development beyond the plane he first flew in the
Twenties and even more generations beyond the "flying coffin"
Uncle Sydney flew in the dogfights of World War I.

Before his first plane, though, Pop had a motorcycle, a Harley-
Davidson. No question, Pop was a daredevil. He didn't wait for a

plane, or tigers in the jungle, to get his thrills. He found plenty right at home on his Harley. In the winter of 1919, for example, he rode it across Long Island Sound, which had frozen solid. Ships could not make it through to the East River, but Pop could carry out the insane feat of riding his motorcycle from Glen Cove to Rye, miles away on the north side of the Sound.

Pop bought his first plane in the 1920s. Aviation rules were lax and, without getting arrested, he flew his plane under the East River bridges between Manhattan and Queens. Late in the decade, he found out where Mom was staying on a lake in Maine with her friend Julie. While the two women were peacefully canoeing on the lake, they saw a small plane approaching. Getting as low as he could Pop buzzed the lake and threw bottles from the cockpit into the water. The bottles were stuffed with marriage proposals and vows of undying love for Mom… they were married the following year.

Pop also liked cars. After the war he started a foreign-car business, which he, and sometimes Mom, ran when Sam and I were growing up. Pop had liked cars since he was a teenager early in the century. In about 1915 he had bought a two-seater Orient Buckboard—with a tiller rather than a steering wheel—which he drove up the front drive to the Big House. He had bought it to impress Muffy, the girl next door, but Muffy was too scared to take a ride in it.

Grandfather Brewster had done well in the world of the horse and carriage. He had little interest in the new motor vehicles and did not own one. Neither he nor Frederick, the coachman, knew how to drive a car. When Grandfather Brewster traveled from Manhattan to the Big House at the beginning of the summer, he went by carriage; when he commuted to the City from Glen Cove, he drove a tandem pair of horses to the Glen Cove–

Nassau train station. He sat in a two-seater holding the reins with Frederick beside him. After Grandfather Brewster had boarded the train for New York, Frederick brought the rig and the horses back to the stables at the East Cottage. Family lore has it that the train conductor could set his watch and the train's departure time by Grandfather Brewster's arrival every morning, just in time to board for Manhattan.

Thus, as Pop drove his new motor vehicle up to the front door of the Big House, the paternal automotive skeptic was standing on the front steps, hair parted in the middle, mustache bristling, his pocket watch and gold watch chain stretched across the dark blue vest that covered his rotund chest and belly. As the disapproving father observed Pop's modern vehicle coming up the driveway, he noted some similarities with a horse-drawn buggy: except for the tiller and small engine, the body of Pop's Orient Buckboard was hard to distinguish from the tandem horse-drawn rig Grandfather Brewster drove at high speed to the Long Island Railroad station. Notwithstanding the similarity, nothing about this modern motor-driven vehicle impressed the patriarch. When Pop pulled up to the Big House, Grandfather Brewster announced, "A fool and his money are soon parted." Coincidentally, this was one of the proverbs in Henry Peacham's book about how to make and keep "mony."

But Pop was from a new generation. He spent a lifetime in love with the automobile. When Sam and I were little, and Pop was in the business of importing and selling small foreign cars, a particular favorite was a Spanish racing car called a Pegaso. When Pop was away and Mom wasn't looking my older brother, Tom, back from college for one of the vacations, borrowed a Pegaso from Pop's dealership and took me on a hair-raising ride on the back roads of Oyster Bay.

Pop enjoyed new foreign cars and old cars that looked like motorized carriages. At one point he owned a 1919 Brewster Automobile, with basket-weave coachwork and patent-leather fenders. It had an open front seat for the chauffeur and a rear passenger cab—dark green with a cream-colored basket-weave and a black leather top. Inside the cab were upholstered seats, a flower vase on a bracket, and a phone-like device for speaking with the chauffeur. Between the patent-leather front fenders and the engine, headlights were mounted on either side of the hood. It was an amazing machine and Pop kept it in one of the garages behind the cottages.

The 1919 Brewster was manufactured by distant cousins in Long Island City, after they switched from making carriages first to car bodies, and then to a very expensive automobile in collaboration with a motor and chassis maker called Delaunay-Belleville. With its open chauffeur's seat and fancy coachwork the car was clearly a "horseless carriage" for the rich. To illustrate the car's desirability, before the First World War and the Russian Revolution, our cousins' catalog featured a photograph of Tsar Nicholas II, his chauffeur, and the Tsar's family proudly traveling in a Brewster-Delaunay-Belleville.

Pop drove Sam and me to church in the Brewster and we also joined him when he drove it in an antique-car parade before a baseball game in Yankee Stadium. The Brewster stalled in the middle of the parade and Pop had to get out and use the crank to get it going again.

Pop's love for planes and cars was fun for Sam and me, but I don't think I ever loved Pop or appreciated him more than when I was suspended in my senior year at Princeton. Lane, one of my roommates, and I were arrested by the Campus Police late one spring night. Having little to do between exams and graduation, we drank epic quantities of beer and were then inspired to see how many campus street lamps we could break with stones on our way back from bar to dorm after midnight. The Campus Police caught us in the act. The next morning, Dean Lippincott suspended both of us and we were ordered to leave campus and return home, Lane to Philadelphia and me to Glen Cove.

Dean Lippincott made it clear that in order to graduate, Lane and I had to explain ourselves to our fathers and persuade them to sign letters acknowledging our confessions of wrongdoing and requesting reinstatement in the university as well as permission to graduate with the class of '64. The Dean told us, "You are lucky I am not planning to notify your law schools." Lane was going to NYU Law School; I had been accepted by Columbia and was on the waiting list at Harvard.

We went home. In Philadelphia, Lane received a stern lecture from his father, a serious Quaker, who told him that he had disgraced the family. In Glen Cove, the reaction from Pop was very different. Pop had long been concerned that I was overly serious and studious; I had many friends but I was a straight arrow to the point that made Pop worry.

I returned to the Big House and told Pop I needed to tell him about something that had happened.

We went into the library and sat down beneath the monumental engraving of our ancestor, William Brewster, standing on Plymouth Rock in 1620, his gaze heavenward, his arms uplifted. I made the confession without which I could neither graduate nor go to law school. Pop listened in silence. Elder Brewster stood on Plymouth Rock and made his presence felt from the wall above.

After a painful pause, Pop smiled and said, "I was hoping you would loosen up." He then spent about an hour telling me about his Harley-Davidson and his days at Princeton, where he himself had, at last, been able to cut loose, free from any fear of criticism from Grandfather Brewster.

My first wife, Michelle, and I were married in 1964 in Brussels, Belgium, where Michelle's family lived. Michelle was half Belgian and half American and spoke French, English, and a combination of the two, which she and her two sisters called "Franglais." The mix of languages was the product of Michelle's family background: Her mother was from Boston; her father a Belgian whose own mother had moved to Belgium from Indiana at the turn of the 20th century after marrying a Belgian banker in an Indiana wedding ceremony. One of the guests at the wedding was the groom's family doctor who had been asked to attend in case of Indian attack.

Michelle went to junior college in Hackettstown, New Jersey, near Princeton, and we met during a college weekend at the beginning of my senior year. Our wedding in Brussels was on September 1. There was no time for a honeymoon and barely enough time to fly home to start my first year of law school, either at Columbia, where I had been accepted, or Harvard, where I was on the waiting list. When we landed in New York, I learned that I had been accepted by Harvard and Michelle and I moved to Cambridge for the duration. After I graduated in June 1967, we moved back to Glen Cove and into the West Cottage, so that I could study for the July bar exam.

Pop lived for another two years. The doctors never could diagnose or treat his decades-long depression. Psychiatric hospitals, electric-shock treatments, and a long stay at a ranch in Tucson, Arizona, did him no good. I missed him when he was away and still have the arrowhead he brought back from Tucson for me.

After Grandmother Brewster died in the late Thirties, Pop gave Mom half of what he had inherited. When Pop's depression deepened, Mom used some of the money to buy an 18th-century farmhouse and farm near Norwich, Connecticut. She tried to persuade Pop to move there, sell the Big House, and retire to a life with less stress. But Pop could not tear himself away from Glen Cove and so the Connecticut farm sat there, unused, until Mom sold it after he died.

They stayed in the Big House and Pop continued to drink heavily. Mom kept telling him that self-medication was going to damage his health and would not cure his depression or whatever undiagnosed mental or neurological issues afflicted him. In 1969, Pop suffered a second stroke brought on by smoking two or more packs of Lucky Strikes a day and drinking gin martinis from late morning on.

If Mom was ever mad at him, she might call Pop "Warren," but these were rare moments. Usually she called him "Chick." They loved each other, even if their 40 years of marriage was not what the 30-year-old Mom signed up for when he buzzed the lake in Maine where she was canoeing at the end of the Roaring Twenties.

A few months before Pop's second stroke, Mom had said to him, "Chick, if you keep doing this, something awful is going to happen." That morning in 1969, Mom walked up to Pop as he was smoking a Lucky and making his first martini of the day. Something was not right. He gripped the pantry sink and said, "awful, awful," before collapsing. He never said another word and died on the second floor of the Big House six agonizing months later in August 1969.

For the last 10 or so years of his life, Pop was retired from business and got back into sailing, a passion he had shared with Sydney, growing up in the summers on Long Island Sound. Pop introduced Mom to sailing when they were first married. About 10 years before he died, he had a 35-ft wooden yawl built, in which he and Mom sailed together until his stroke. He named the yacht *Rose Wood*, Mom's mother's maiden name. I know of no one else who named his sailboat after his mother-in-law.

I loved my grandmother, Omy, but I'm not sure she deserved Pop's tribute. Gramps, Thomas Darrah, was a West Pointer, a career army officer. Omy's father, William Maxwell Wood, went to Annapolis and her grandfather, also William Maxwell Wood, was a doctor who became the US Navy's first Surgeon General. In Omy's eyes, Pop and his family were nothing more than Ohio farmers who had left the land and soiled their hands in commerce. Mom had married beneath her—unless you equated class with money, which Omy did not. Omy and Gramps had no money. Her father died a young and penniless navy lieutenant and Gramps was an orphan from Kansas, who escaped the Plains by going to West Point, getting shot at in a number of wars, and eventually becoming a General. When I knew Gramps, he and Omy lived in a rent-controlled apartment on 82nd Street—an address chosen primarily for its proximity to the largest number of their grandchildren.

Pop created and funded a trust to make his in-laws' lives on 82nd Street more comfortable, since they had nothing besides Gramps's military pension. It was a good deed that did not go unpunished and when Omy moved into the Big House after suffering a number of falls in the apartment, she brought her lack of appreciation for Pop with her. And yet, despite it all, it was for her that Pop named his last sailboat.

When Pop died, Mom was, for once, overwhelmed, and I was sent as messenger to Omy. I went into her room and said, "I've got bad news, Omy. Pop is dead."

"That's not bad news, Richard, it is good news."

Omy's comment may not have been a reflection of her contempt for Pop, but rather of her compassion for Mom and even for Pop's release from a speechless and joyless existence, but I heard only the critical mother-in-law. I never spoke to her again. The grandmother I loved, but was angry with, died two months later, well into her 90s, just before Michelle gave birth to our first child, Sylvia.

Many said that Sylvia was the spitting image of Omy.

CHAPTER 8.

The Gramps I Knew
(1941–1955)

> If you save and lay up but 12 pennies a day, it
> comes to more than 109 pounds in 3 years. If
> you save in time, Apparel & Mony [sic] 2 shil-
> lings a day, in 21 years it makes 766 pounds.
>
> *William Stoughton flyleaf note*

BEFORE SIGNING death warrants for the condemned in the
Salem witchcraft trials, William Stoughton applied his principles
of obsessive thrift to become one of the richest men in the English North American colonies. Grandfather Brewster would have
related to Stoughton's interest in making money.

Gramps, my mother's father, was a very different man in terms
of both his life and his values. Born into poverty in Kansas, when
he died in 1955, he was in approximately the same financial condi-
tion in which he had begun his life's journey. He had a successful
army career, which led to medals, campaign ribbons, and promo-
tions; it did not lead to riches.

When Gramps saw me throw my coat onto a chair inside the
front door of the Big House instead of hanging it up, he said, "You
won't get into West Point that way." West Point had freed Gramps
from his life as a penniless orphan in Kansas. I visited West Point
with him, Mom, and Sam to watch a parade of cadets and to
spend time with Col. Red Reeder, West Point's athletic director,

who had married Gramps's Kansas niece, Dorothea. I remember Col. Reeder walking with a limp because he had lost a leg after being wounded on D-Day in Normandy.

Gramps did not talk about the battles and wars in which he had fought. Indeed, the most military thing I ever saw him do was position himself, like an MP, next to the front door of the Big House in order to confiscate water pistols from my friends as they came in for my birthday party. My friends meekly turned over their weapons to General Darrah.

I knew that Gramps had been in many battles in a number of wars and lived to be tall, trim, and still fit at 80. Mom came from the same stock and lived to be over 100.

In contrast, Pop's father, Grandfather Brewster, made a great deal of money in business and died before he was 70. His wealth did not bring either happiness or long life to his sons, Sydney and Pop. The whispers about Sydney's murder-suicide and Pop's depression, his stays in psychiatric hospitals, and the evil spirits that I imagined haunting my family, all had a deeply emotional significance for me. Lesson number one: there was bad blood in the Brewster family. Lesson number two: fighting battles and dodging bullets like Gramps were safer than being in business. In my psyche, money and the making of money were somehow connected to Peacham's curse.

With Pop often away, Gramps loomed large in my life. As long as he was alive he overshadowed Omy, at least in my eyes.

Gramps had first seen Rose Wood as she was getting off a train. He told us that he took one look at her and said, "That's the girl I am going to marry." After he returned from the Spanish-American War, where he won the first of his Silver Stars for courage under fire, he and Rose (Omy to me) were married in Washington, DC, in April 1899 in a double wedding with Omy's sister Jeanne and her groom, Joe Tracy, also a lieutenant. Gramps and Joe were in full uniform. Jeanne carried white lilies of the valley and Omy carried roses.

When Omy had introduced Gramps to her sister she told him that there had been a Jeanne or Jennie or Jean in every generation of her family since Jeanne Josephine DeGilsey Fadeuilhe and her husband Georges moved from Toulouse in the south of France, first to Washington and then to New Orleans, early in the 19th century.

Omy was proud of her French ancestry, but whenever she got onto the topic of her ancestry, Gramps would say she was really descended from French pirates, while he was descended from Irish kings. He was joking on both counts. Georges Fadeuilhe was not a pirate. In business with his brother in Toulouse, Georges moved to Washington to sell French carpeting—our government buildings had been destroyed when the British burned the capital, in reprisal for our having set Toronto on fire, and as the rebuild took hold under Presidents Madison and Monroe, French carpet was in demand.

The truth or fiction of pirates and kings aside, I owe a debt I can never repay to the fact that Gramps was an orphan. His mother had already died when his father was killed in a gunfight. Gramps and his brother and sister were taken in by relatives in Kansas. As a result of such suffering at an early age, Gramps made it part of his life's work to ensure that none of his children or grandchildren would experience the loneliness that he had felt as an orphan. One of the ways in which he expressed this was to use his fine woodworking skills to make one gift after another for each of us.

Gramps learned woodworking from Victor Strozak, a cabinetmaker from New York who was his driver in the Philippines—where Gramps was stationed at different times during his military career. Working with Strozak, and surrounded by mahogany forests,

Gramps became a passionate woodworker, eventually making things for himself and Omy and gifts for his children and grandchildren that ranged from dining room sets to doll's furniture, carriage models, ship models, silver chests, tool chests, and toy chests. He carried his passion into retirement and supplemented his pension by making carriage models for museums.

Gramps was always making things for me. First there was the toy chest at the foot of my bed, then a varnished wooden toolbox with brass corners and my initials, RWB, in splendid block lettering on the lid. He made three 36-inch-long working model sailboats, in different colors for Tom, Sam, and me. Their beautifully varnished decks were meticulously laid with individual planks. My boat was yellow above the waterline and black below, with a fine pinstripe between. We sailed our sloops, rigged by Gramps with sails made from white shirt cloth, in Long Island Sound. For my sister, Isabel, Gramps made a three-story doll house with rooms he furnished in the style of the 18th and 19th centuries—tables, chairs, beds, miniature mirrors, and other furnishings, all handmade, no kits.

In the library Gramps helped me find interesting things to paste in my scrapbook. He did the same for Sam. Taking the *Encyclopedia Britannica* from the library shelves, he looked up the answers to questions we had about things like headhunters in the Philippine rain forests and their shrunken heads. I truly believed that headhunters stalked the rain forests when Gramps was in the Philippines. He also read to us from Kipling's *Jungle Books*, Cooper's *The Last of the Mohicans* and Mark Twain's *A Connecticut Yankee in King Arthur's Court*. Through them all we were wide-eyed, but in particular Twain's Connecticut Yankee, Hank Morgan, made a lasting impression. In his time-travel to Camelot, Hank Morgan brought modern knowledge of guns and gunpowder.

8. *The Gramps I Knew (1941–1955)*

Making a field trip out of the tale, one day Gramps walked with us from his apartment at 122 East 82nd Street to the Metropolitan Museum of Art on Fifth Avenue. There he pointed to what looked like a bullet hole in a spectacular suit of armor in the museum's armory collection. Gramps invited us to consider how the bullet hole got there. "Do you think Hank Morgan put it there?"

Gramps could not stop making things like our working sailboat models. Being youngest, mine came after those made for Tom and Sam. I couldn't wait. One day, when he was close to finishing it, he and Omy were taking a nap in their bedroom. So eager was I to have him get back to my boat project that I ran up and down the hallway past the bedroom door. It did not have the desired effect. Gramps poked his head out and spoke to me sharply—something along the lines of "Stop that, Richard," or maybe, "Richard, stop that this minute." I don't recall Gramps ever getting really mad; when he made a mistake while woodworking in my presence, he often said "Ffffffff…" eventually voicing the word "feathers." Perhaps because of his normally mild manner, I was stung by that rebuke in the hallway.

Gramps's retirement workshop started out in the basement of the apartment building where he and Omy lived. Eventually, the building needed the basement space and Gramps moved his shop to the playhouse that he had built for Isabel by the edge of the trees between the Big House and Smuggler's Lane. Isabel was away at Smith College and had long lost interest in the playhouse. After its conversion to a woodworking shop, Sam and I would watch Gramps use the miniature lathe, drill press, and a host of tools to work his magic. On the lathe Gramps turned wood and brass into beautiful shapes for his miniature furniture and models.

In September 1954, Sam went away to St. Paul's School and Mom became more involved in Pop's automobile business. Pop saw the benefits of small European cars, but the Long Island suburbs were still devoted to giant gas-guzzlers with fins. As a means to make money Brewster Automobiles was a struggle and Mom and Pop were often away from the house either because of the faltering business or Pop's ill health.

That fall, Gramps sensed that his youngest grandchild was lonely in the Big House. He helped me to fill the void by improving my woodworking skills. He sketched shop drawings for me, so that I could make a small 18th-century-style tea table with a round top and fluted pedestal, with three legs at the base of the pedestal, bending their knees to put their 18th-century-style feet to the floor. Gramps had made a more elaborate full-sized mahogany tea table for Mom and Pop, which stood in the library next to the couch where they had cocktails and listened to Paul Harvey telling the "rest of the story" behind the day's news. It was a beautiful piece of furniture—around the top, Gramps had carved the rim with identical, repeating swags, reminiscent of a perfectly crimped crust on an apple pie—Mom called it the "piecrust" table.

My smaller table was of simpler design with neither a tilt top nor the piecrust edge. Instead, Gramps drew a simple fluted edge—more achievable for a seventh grader. I planned to make the table in Mr. Gunn's shop class at school as a present for Mom. I thought she could put it next to the *chaise longue* in her and Pop's bedroom, where she sat next to the window and read one book after another, fiction and non-fiction, history and romance.

Sam and I had watched Gramps in his shop. He taught us how to use a chisel and lathe, how to hold the chisel with care so that it did not catch in the lathe and fly out of our hands, at great risk to fingers and eyes. Already schooled by Gramps, I took easily to the lathe in Mr. Gunn's shop class. With Mr. Gunn's guidance, Gramps's shop drawings, and a few more consults with Gramps,

I was coming along well with the table when school closed for Christmas vacation and we headed to our house in Vermont to ski. I would have the table finished sometime that winter and would stain it to look like mahogany well ahead of Mom's June birthday.

Gramps never saw the finished table. One day at the end of January, Mom was not home when I got back from school. Mrs. Hagstrom, "Hagsie" to me, who sometimes worked in the Big House, welcomed me when I got off the bus. She told me that Mom had gone to the City because Gramps had had a heart attack. She must have spoken with Mom on the phone later, for it was Hagsie who told me that Gramps had died.

The next few days were a blur. I remember going to a skating party after school, possibly the next day. But I don't remember skating. I was in no mood to skate or celebrate.

I remember that Omy, Mom, and I went on the train to Washington for Gramps's funeral at Arlington National Cemetery. I don't remember if Sam came down from St. Paul's, nor do I remember if Pop was with us. I am reasonably sure that neither Isabel nor Tom was there. I remember the Arlington Chapel and horses pulling Gramps's coffin away from the chapel on a funeral wagon after the service. I do not remember if we went to the grave to see the coffin lowered into the ground. Some things are vivid in my memory: soldiers in a line fired guns in a salute. There was a saddled but riderless horse with boots placed backwards in the stirrups, representing the soldier who would never ride again. I remember feeling a great sense of loneliness after the funeral and on the train back to New York. Gramps was gone and Sam was away at school. The Big House felt very big and very empty.

Omy gave me Gramps's medals—two Silver Stars, a Bronze Star, and many campaign ribbons, as well as his 1895 West Point class ring and letters that Douglas MacArthur had written to

him from the Pacific during the Second World War. I knew that
Gramps had been MacArthur's chief of staff between the wars;
based on his incredible attention to detail as a woodworker, I am
sure he was a valued chief of staff. He and MacArthur had always
stayed in touch. After the war MacArthur asked Gramps to manage his campaign for President, but Gramps turned him down.
Gramps had already had one heart attack and did not want the
stress of a political campaign. I do not recall ever having a political
conversation with Gramps and so have no idea whether he agreed
with MacArthur's politics or not.

When Sam eventually came home for vacation after Gramps
died, we used the lathe in the woodworking shop to turn and shape
heavy brass rods into miniature cannons. We drilled our cannon
barrels in the press, made touch holes for ignition and mounted
the cannons on gun carriages that we fashioned from Philippine
mahogany scraps we found in the bins under the workbench. With
gunpowder from firecrackers and kitchen matches, Sam and I shot
spitballs from our cannons. When no one was looking, the library
became our military theater.

I have no memory of talking with Mom about Gramps's death,
but some time later she took me to her framing shop in Sea Cliff
and had the shop make a glazed shadow box for his medals.

I have worn Gramps's West Point ring for more than 60 years.

CHAPTER 9.

Flashback — The Shootout
That Made Gramps an Orphan
(1897)

There are others again…who are easily fetch'd
and drawn in by decayed and crafty knaves…

The Worth Of A Penny, p. 14

I IMAGINE Gramps's mother dying when he was a toddler and his father, Sam Jones Darrah, being killed by a villain in a six-gun shootout on a dusty street in Kansas. Family lore had it that Sam Jones Darrah must have been ambushed by a "decayed and crafty knave"—to use Henry Peacham's words. It is impossible that Sam Jones Darrah could have been killed in a fair fight, because no one was faster on the draw, no one could out-shoot him—such was the heart of the story that came down in the family. It was largely fiction.

The reality of Gramps's father's life and death must have been painful to Gramps, and he significantly altered and fabricated the facts before passing the story along. As is so often the case, the truth was somewhat more prosaic.

Gramps's mother died in 1887 when Gramps was 14. Gramps's father was a horseman who transported things like whiskey and hams westward by horse and mule pack trains over the Santa Fe trail. After the Civil War the new railroads drove the pack trains into extinction, and Sam Jones Darrah's thoughts turned to ranching.

Darrah passed on his love for horses to his son. Gramps bought his first horse from Plains Indians trading at Leavenworth and his skills as a horseman were important to him. Though a poor boy from Kansas, Gramps would later become Captain of the Army polo team. In World War I he was involved in the painful task of supplying the American Army with horses, many of which died horrible deaths on the front in the Meuse-Argonne offensive.

By the time I started school after World War II, the role of the horse in both military life and civilian transportation had vanished, but I remember Gramps listening to horse races on the radio and talking about why a particular horse was his favorite.

Soon after Gramps's mother died, Sam Jones Darrah disappeared from his son's life. He eventually remarried, and not long before Gramps graduated from West Point, moved across the Rockies to California. He did not attend the graduation and Gramps changed his middle name from Schuyler to Walter, the name of the Leavenworth doctor, Dr. Walter, who was married to Gramps's aunt and provided a home for Gramps and his siblings after their mother's death.

Sam Jones Darrah's abandonment of his children and subsequent remarriage must have been painful for Gramps. There may have been a feeling of shame or even responsibility. For whatever reason, in Gramps's version of Sam Jones Darrah's death, the Kansas horseman went down in a hail of bullets on a dusty street immediately after his wife died. As children we all believed that this shocking event had happened when Gramps and his sister and brother were very young.

There was some truth behind Gramps's story. There was a shootout. It may well not have been a fair fight, but it was not on a dusty street in Kansas. Sam Jones Darrah was killed on the edge of the desert in California where he had moved with Mary Kennerly, his new wife. He had bought a ranch in a place called Snow Creek, a few miles from Palm Springs. He died, in 1897, in a gunfight with his neighbor during a dispute over rights to the water in the creek which then ran through both of their properties.

For more than 60 years, the shootout that made Gramps an orphan drew me like a magnet—wherever it took place. At first I wanted to find that dusty street in Kansas. Then, when I learned from a Missouri cousin that the gunfight had taken place at Snow Creek in California, I was determined to go there. In 2019 I finally made it.

For the second year running Barbara, my second wife, was attending a conference at the Anaheim Hilton. My quest to go to Snow Creek had been prevented the previous year because of wildfires between Riverside and Palm Springs but now, in 2019, the fires were gone. At last I made it to Snow Creek and filled in many of the details of Sam Jones Darrah's death.

Sam was a combative Irishman. He nailed a sign to a post or tree along Snow Creek, which read, "THIS WATER BELONGS TO S.J. DARRAH." His neighbor, Milner, had sold him the ranch on Snow Creek, but blocked the water Sam needed by putting in a sluice on land that Milner kept upstream. In Sam's eyes Milner was a swindler who sold him useable ranchland and then turned off the critical life-sustaining faucet. Mary Kennerly, who had come with Sam from Kansas, was pregnant and about to give birth to their child. If the swindler had his way, Sam would not be able to make a living for his new family.

To make matters worse, Milner was negotiating with a syndicate, possibly with the intent to divert the water from Snow Creek entirely. Sam saw both Milner and the syndicate as "decayed and crafty knaves"—to use Henry Peacham's words. They had "fetch'd and drawn in" Sam. He had to stop them.

Going to court did not resolve the dispute, and Sam ordered his hired man to rip out the sluice. The hired man did so, but Milner quickly rebuilt. He threatened Sam's hired man, who refused to risk ripping out the sluice a second time.

Filled with rage, Sam took matters into his own hands. With his lever-action rifle, he headed up the boulder-strewn slope along Snow Creek toward the sluice. As he approached it, Milner stepped out from behind a boulder and killed him. Nine balls of lead buckshot fired from Milner's shotgun ripped through Sam's chest.

In Milner's ensuing murder trial, the prosecution's theory was that Milner was waiting behind the boulders and ambushed Sam as he approached the sluice. At trial, Milner claimed that Sam fired his rifle first and that Milner had acted in self-defense. Indeed, according to the crime-scene investigation, Sam's rifle, found next to his body, had fired at least one shot. Thus the issue was clear: Had Milner acted in self-defense or had he ambushed Sam and then taken the rifle from Sam's dead hand, fired it, and replaced it next to Sam's body to stage a claim of self-defense?

The jury had to weigh the circumstantial evidence and Milner's credibility as his own defense witness. The jury found Milner guilty of murder. But Milner had a good lawyer or perhaps friends in the right places—on appeal the court reversed the murder conviction on a technicality. At retrial, the jury again found Milner guilty, but this time of manslaughter.

Again the conviction was reversed on a technicality. A third trial ensued. The jury was deadlocked. A fourth trial followed and Milner was acquitted. The charlatan-murderer's powerful friends and lawyers kept the legal system churning until the killer got away with it. Sam was buried in an unmarked grave in Riverside, California, and after his death, Mary Kennerly gave birth to his daughter.

In August 2019, some 122 years later, I stood in the desert heat among the boulders where Sam Jones Darrah was killed. There was not a drop of water where Snow Creek had once flowed down from the mountains. Perhaps, in 1897, there were trees along the creek, but today there is neither tree nor any sign of life other than some cactus. The creek bed is still visible and the same boulders are still scattered across the slope. I stood among them in the shimmering and oppressive August heat as I thought of the moment when Milner stepped out from behind one of the boulders and killed Sam Jones Darrah.

CHAPTER 10.

Bay of Pigs on Bicycles
(1956)

KEEP IN MIND THAT BOLSHEVISM
IS ENEMY NUMBER ONE.

Telegram from Marc Sevastopoulo
8:19 a.m., November 5, 1968,
Election Day

MY OLDEST FRIEND, Dimitri Sevastopoulo, is the son of Marc
Sevastopoulo, always Mr. Sevastopoulo to me. Both before and
after I graduated from law school in 1967, I enjoyed talking about
history and politics with Mr. Sevastopoulo, whether we agreed or
not. He sent me the above-quoted telegram about Bolshevism just
after eight o'clock on the morning of Election Day 1968. Later in
the day the counted votes sent Richard Nixon to the White House
on a platform of law and order fueled by the year's traumatic events.
During the course of 1968 the fabric of life in the United States
had been torn apart by urban riots, the assassinations of Martin
Luther King and Robert Kennedy, and Civil Rights and Vietnam
War protests. In my conversation with Mr. Sevastopoulo the day
before the election, I argued that the underlying causes of the protests and riots must be addressed. Mr. Sevastopoulo thought that I
had been possessed by leftist demons from Harvard. I was his son's
oldest friend and he wanted to rescue me from the errors of my
youth and indiscretion. He sent me the telegram to emphasize the

83

paramount danger of the "Bolshevism" that he saw in the country's chaotic events.

Urban unrest of any kind raised the specter of "Bolshevism" in Mr. Sevastopoulo's mind. It was deeply personal to him. More than a decade older than my parents, he grew up in a beautiful house in Odessa on the Black Sea. As a young officer in the Russian Army, he was assigned to the Tsar's Palace Guard. After the Revolution erupted, he made his way through a country in chaos back to his family home in Odessa. From there he escaped with his mother to Istanbul—Constantinople as he knew it. From there he returned to Russia to fight with Tsarist forces in the failed effort to defeat the "Bolsheviks" and restore the Tsar to power. Mr. Sevastopoulo's final escape from Russia was in the dead of winter across the frozen Black Sea near Odessa. He fled on foot while the Red Army fired artillery and mortar shells onto the frozen sea in an effort to either shoot or drown the remnants of the Tsarist forces before they could be evacuated by rescue ships at the edge of the ice.

Dimitri's father survived. He moved to the United States and married Dimitri's mother, a Russian princess, after first marrying and divorcing an American heiress. He had left Russia with nothing but his wits and charm. But he was an unstoppable force. I had heard the tales of his escape from Russia and the evils of Bolshevism since Dimitri and I met in the second grade at Green Vale School in Glen Head, a few miles from where Dimitri and I both lived in the small city of Glen Cove.

In his new life in the United States Mr. Sevastopoulo became a sales representative for an importer-distributor of French champagne and liqueurs. In his travels around the US selling champagne and liqueurs, he sometimes purchased fireworks, which he gave to Dimitri and which Dimitri shared with me. With those fireworks and the inspirational tales of his father crossing the ice under fire, Dimitri and I were equipped and inspired to carry out our covert operation—the storming of the Soviet Russians' Glen Cove mansion on our bicycles.

"Killenworth," a 40-room mansion on Dosoris Lane, was built in 1912 for George Dupont Pratt, the son of oil refiner and Rockefeller partner, Charles Pratt. In 1951, the robber baron's house was purchased by the Soviet Union as a retreat for the Soviet delegation to the United Nations. Killenworth was the ideal target for two boys determined to avenge Soviet Russian misdeeds. What we did there could have gotten us arrested or worse.

In the second grade, our teacher, Miss Cummings, was quick to identify Dimitri and me as troublemakers and it was she who made sure we were separated as we moved into the third grade. In my third-grade class, there was a new kid named Bobby who came to Green Vale from a public school in Huntington. Bobby had great worldly knowledge. Somewhere between the classroom, the hallway, and the boys' room on the second floor of the lower school building, Bobby shared some of that worldly knowledge, graphically explaining to me how babies are made.

As soon as I could, I passed along this important information to Dimitri. He looked at me in disbelief. His mother was born the Princess Cantacuzene. To me, she was "Mrs. Sevastopoulo," to my parents, "Erze." She was very unassuming about her heritage, but she surely looked like a beautiful princess. More beautiful than Audrey Hepburn, more beautiful even than Miss Cummings.

Shocked by my newfound information regarding babies, Dimitri reacted with skepticism, "Well, maybe that's how *your* mother made *you*." Surely no Russian princess could ever do what Bobby described. Given his origins, perhaps Dimitri thought that he and I might have been conceived and entered the world in different ways. His reaction did not affect our friendship.

Dimitri and I were best friends. Inspired by Westerns at the movie theater in Glen Cove, we became blood brothers by using a pocketknife to scratch our thumbs and pressing our bloody thumb pads together under the ginkgo tree at the end of the front drive to the Big House.

We were boys and we had bicycles and the "b" in "bicycles" came in the alphabet and in our lives before the "g" in "girls." By the time Sam went away to boarding school I had my own bike. My allowance was just 25 cents a week—not nearly enough for a bike—and I had to talk Pop into laying out the money. It was a hard sell. My argument that all the other kids, including Dimitri, already had bikes, did not cut much ice. It took some time, but Pop eventually gave in.

With a rag, a soft cloth, and some automotive wax I polished the dark-green fenders and frame of my Raleigh bicycle. Now I could quickly reach the other side of Glen Cove where Dimitri lived on Cedar Swamp Road and he could easily bike to Crescent Beach Road. From either of our homes we could bike to the homes of the rest of our rat pack in Glen Head, Locust Valley, Brookville, Westbury, and beyond.

Dimitri and I continued to be the troublemakers that Miss Cummings had identified in the second grade. When it came to troublemaking Dimitri claimed that I was the ringleader, and I concede that on at least one occasion this was true.

One day, Dimitri bicycled over to see me at the Big House. My mother had laid out some of her favorite possessions—Lalique crystal birds—on the dining room table. They were to be part of an arrangement for a flower show in Locust Valley. The same day, not far from the dining room table, oranges were piled in a bowl on the kitchen counter, waiting to be squeezed for juice the next morning. In turn, the bowl of oranges was next to the squeezing device—a ridged ceramic cone sticking up out of a dish. To extract the juice, you cut the orange in half, pressed and turned it on the ridged cone, and watched as the stream of juice ran down the ridges into the dish.

I looked at the ceramic cone. I looked at Dimitri's nose. Dimitri's nose was worthy of the Imperial Russian aristocracy. His nose also looked like the ceramic cone in the orange juicer. An idea was born: I would squeeze a half orange on Dimitri's nose. I told Dimitri. He thought it a bad idea and ran. I chased after him around the kitchen and then into the dining room with a half orange in my right hand. We went around the table until I caught up with him near the Lalique birds. We fell onto the table, which was supported by pedestals. The table tipped and the Lalique birds slid off and crashed to the floor. At least one was broken beyond repair, another was badly chipped. Hearing the noise, Mom ran into the dining room and burst into tears. This brought Pop to the scene. He pointed to the front door and sent Dimitri packing. Through the dining room windows I could see the wheels of Dimitri's bicycle spinning in a blur as he raced away to Cedar Swamp Road. He was exiled from the Big House for a couple of weeks, until after Halloween—our big night of trick-or-treating and teaming up to cause trouble…punishment indeed.

The ban lifted, we were soon bicycling back and forth between our two homes and beyond. We often bicycled on Dosoris Lane towards Bayville and Oyster Bay. A short distance out, we pedaled past the wrought-iron and stone gate of Killenworth, the Soviets' retreat. Dimitri and I had heard that, after the Russians bought the old Pratt mansion, a Pratt family friend, unaware of the sale, had stopped by to visit unannounced. Her chauffeur pulled up in front of the mansion and she walked through the open front door only to be confronted by a giant portrait of Stalin in the staircase rising from the front hall. On hearing the story, Dimitri and I made a mental note: the front door had been left open; Soviet security must be lax.

It was not unusual for us to continue on past Killenworth and even past Morgan's Island, through Lattingtown and along the shore road to Bayville. Bayville had a strip of greasy-spoon beach restaurants selling clams, hot dogs, French fries, sodas, and beer (if you were old enough, which we were not).

Occasionally, we went beyond Bayville over the steep hill and down the other side to Oyster Bay. Better known for Teddy Roosevelt's home, Oyster Bay also had a historic 18th-century building, Raynham Hall, owned by the family of George Washington's spymaster, Robert Townsend, who used the code name Samuel Culper. It was there that I bought a book about George Washington's spies and learned about their use of invisible ink to write between the lines of seemingly innocuous letters. With this methodology they sent information about British troop movements and strength to Washington's headquarters. The seeds of Dimitri's and my covert operation on Dosoris Lane grew from reading about Washington's spies.

We conceived the delusional fantasy that we were going to storm and seize the Russians' mansion on Dosoris Lane. We wanted to avoid detection while we mapped out our plans. Approximating the methods of Washington's spies, we started writing letters from one side of Glen Cove to the other with details of our plan written between the lines in lemon juice. At Dimitri's house on Cedar Swamp Road or my house on Crescent Beach Road, we heated the letters over candles and the invisible messages appeared. It was interesting once, but it was time-consuming and paled quickly. We finalized our planning in person—a bike ride from one side of Glen Cove to the other was faster and easier than lemon juice and candles.

We needed weapons for our raid. We made them with the fireworks that Dimitri's father brought back from his sales trips. We had many boxes of sparklers, but the most useful and dangerous items were cherry bombs and M-80s. The cherry bombs were dusty red and looked like a cherry with a stem-like fuse. The M-80s were short gray explosive cylinders with a fuse sticking up in the middle.

Our preparations quickly became seriously delinquent. We used Scotch tape to wrap BBs around the cherry bombs and M-80s. We had not thought our plan through, but the gist of it was that when bombarded with cherry bombs and M-80s wrapped with Scotch tape and BBs, the Russians would surrender the mansion.

I don't remember whether we converged on Dosoris Lane on our bicycles coming from our respective sides of Glen Cove or launched the operation from one of our houses. In any case we arrived on Dosoris Lane with our bike bags laden with weaponry. We reached the wrought-iron gate at the beginning of the long driveway to the mansion. To all outward appearances security was lax, just as we had hoped—the gate was open. We biked through and up the drive.

We did not have time to park our bikes and walk up the steps to the mansion's front door. There must have been some kind of sensor in the driveway that sounded an alarm inside the house. When we reached the front of the mansion, the door was open— as we might have hoped—but standing within the opening was a bearded Russian giant. He scowled at us and with his arm outstretched pointed back towards the gate on Dosoris Lane. He said something loud in Russian that I did not understand. I don't think Dimitri understood it either. Like others in the post-revolutionary Russian diaspora, Dimitri and his family spoke French, not Russian, at home. Nevertheless, the Russian giant's message was clear.

We were to turn around and ride straight back out. We did so. Our covert operation thus ended in abject failure—a juvenile Gallipoli, a Bay of Pigs on bicycles.

Though we were unscathed, our failed mission left us with a problem. Our bike bags were full of unused cherry bombs and BB-enhanced M-8os. We had to dispose of them. I had a tackle box with hooks and fishing line I used for catching snappers near the surface of the water, and lead sinkers used for flounders on the sandy bottom off Crescent Beach. We decided to weight the cherry bombs and M-8os with lead sinkers and thus convert them into depth charges that we could throw into Mrs. Luckenbach's pond at the end of Crescent Beach Road.

We headed back to the Big House to find the tackle box. We wrapped the cherry bombs and M-8os with sinkers and more Scotch tape and biked down Smuggler's Lane to the bottom of the hill, walking through the woods to Mrs. Luckenbach's pond. I don't remember who had the matches and who pitched the explosives into the pond, but we got the job done. The cherry bombs were duds—their explosive charges did not survive immersion in pond water, but in contrast, the M-8os worked like a charm, sinking to the bottom of the pond and exploding, sending great geysers of water into the air. This not only disturbed and annoyed Mrs. Luckenbach's ducks and swans, it attracted the attention of her gardener, who came running in the direction of the pond with a shotgun. We saw him before he saw us and disappeared through the woods, back to our bicycles on Smuggler's Lane and so up the hill to the Big House.

In many ways our attempt to seize the Soviet mansion and the subsequent disposal of the M-8os and cherry bombs were resounding successes: Neither of us blew off any fingers; we were not shot by the bearded Russian giant or by Mrs. Luckenbach's gardener; we were not arrested by the Glen Cove Police or the FBI.

Sixty years later, 10 days after the 2016 Presidential election, in which the Russians were known to have meddled, I turned 75. Dimitri turned 75 a few months later. To celebrate we hosted dinners for each other and a few old friends. Our wives were there, too, but Barbara said the dinners were really stag parties with women tagging along. Stag parties or not, the dinners were treasured hours of celebration with close friends. As the poet Horace said, "The feasts we share with friends the fingers of our heirs will never hold." The evening included toasts to old memories, not least of which was our covert operation on Dosoris Lane.

One month later, the Obama administration blocked the Russians' access to Killenworth, temporarily achieving, without military force or weapons, what Dimitri and I abjectly failed to do with our bicycles, cherry bombs, and M-80s. As the year approached its end I raised a very personal toast to President Obama.

CHAPTER 11.

Getting to Know Omy
(1960–1969)

A rose is a rose is a rose.

Gertrude Stein, 1913

BEFORE SHE MARRIED, Omy was Rose Wood. She was not to become Omy until the late 1920s following the birth of her first grandchild, little Woody. Woody's parents, Jean—my mother's sister—and Woodlief, were living in Germany at the time because of Woodlief's job as a US government economist with the Repurations Commission. And so it was that Rose became known to Woody and all her subsequent grandchildren by one variation or another of the German word for grandmother, Oma.

Omy, Mom, and Jean had lived in the Philippines on at least two of Gramps's three tours of duty there. Mom was born in 1900 and Jean in 1903. When they were very small, they lived in Manila, on the island of Luzon, while Gramps was fighting in the southern islands of Mindanao and Jolo. In Manila earthquakes strong enough to make your home shake were not unusual. The first time they experienced one such event Mom and Jean were scared. Omy was reassuring and dismissive. "It's only an earthquake, children"—earthquakes were just a part of life, nothing to be afraid of; the shaking and rattling always stopped and then you carried on with whatever you had been doing before it started. The

93

will and courage to continue, no matter what, were Omy's most notable traits.

By the time the family came to live in the Philippines, Omy had been through some of life's earthquakes, but none of them had kept her from knowing what she wanted and how she would get it—like sitting on chocolate bars to make them soft, the way she liked them when she was five years old. When it was time for her to go to school, she wanted to learn the things boys learned. Her parents enrolled her in the new Friends' Select School, later called Sidwell Friends, where the Obama girls went. In 1883, the school had just been established as an experiment in offering girls and boys the same education in a co-ed setting.

Omy's parents, Navy Lieutenant William Wood and Jennie Belle West, were married in Washington in 1875. Jeanne was born the following year and Rose in 1878. When they were girls—behind their mother's back at least—Jeanne and Rose called Jennie Belle "Jenny Belly." Lieutenant Wood and Jennie Belle indulged their independent daughters up to a point, but there were limits. When Jeanne was a teenager, she eloped and married her boyfriend without her parents' approval or consent. Lieutenant Wood organized a posse, which rode into the Maryland countryside and brought Jeanne back. The marriage was annulled.

Rose was still a teenager when Gramps first saw her stepping off a train in Buffalo, NY, and knew that she was the girl he was going to marry. I do not know whether they met on that train platform or soon after, but whatever the chronology, their feelings were mutual and they became secretly engaged. Visions of the posse that had ended Jeanne's elopement made Omy and Gramps hesitate in raising the subject of marriage with Omy's father. They never did. Lieutenant William Wood died in December 1897 of Bright's disease in New Rochelle, New York. He was in New York on leave from the navy, absorbed in a pioneering effort to make refrigeration—in particular ice cubes—commercially viable. His untimely death at 47 followed Sam Jones Darrah's death at 55 at Snow Creek, just three months earlier.

The following year, 1898, brought another jarring change in Omy's life. The Spanish-American War broke out and Gramps was sent to Cuba. He returned with a Silver Star for his gallantry under fire and they were married in 1899. A year later, Mom was born.

Gramps was soon back in the Philippines and under fire again, earning his second Silver Star fighting on Luzon. By 1901 he was home again.

Omy's sister had also had a child following their double wedding, little Jeanne. But before the year was over, little Jeanne was dead, the victim of an opiate—laudanum—given by the nanny to make the baby sleep. Arlington was then a family cemetery for military families and baby Jeanne was buried there among her warrior relatives.

Mom's sister, Jean, was born in 1903 and soon Omy and Gramps and the two small girls moved to Manila. In the tropics Omy was struck by a personal blow: With auburn hair and hazel eyes, the 17- or 18-year-old girl with whom Gramps had fallen in love had been very beautiful but in the Philippines she was scourged by a tropical skin disease. For the rest of her life she had disfiguring scars on both sides of her face. Like everything that life threw her way, Omy made little of it. For Gramps, too, the scars did not change how he saw Omy. Indeed, I don't think he ever saw her in any way other than the young girl who stepped off the train in Buffalo.

The disfiguring tropical skin disease was not to be Omy's last ordeal and in 1933 she suffered the greatest blow that can befall any parent—she lost a child. That year, at just 30 years old, Jean died of an infection. Omy never talked about Jean's death, but I am sure that other losses seemed trivial and unimportant in comparison. If ever Omy needed courage to continue, she needed it when Jean died. I did not learn about the devastating impact of Jean's death on Mom until later.

For me, in the years after Gramps died, Omy became her own person. Of course, she always had been her own person, but I was slow to realize it. In 1962, the summer of my sophomore year at college, I lived in her apartment while I had a proofreading job at a Wall Street law firm, Milbank Tweed. I stayed in the small spare room, called a "maid's room." Gramps had used the room, which had a metal-frame army cot, as a study. Over that summer, Omy spoiled me, which often meant starting my day with Grape Nuts and heavy cream before I headed downtown to proofread boring legal documents. Before I could get too fat to fit into Gramps's clothes, Omy gave me both his tuxedo and tweed jacket, which had never left the closet in the maid's room-study. She also gave me his sewing kit from the First World War. She said she could not give me the German Luger pistol that he had picked up on the battlefield in the Meuse-Argonne campaign, because she had already given it to the police. After Gramps died, she heard on the radio about a murder with a handgun in her neighborhood. She called the police to tell them that she had not committed the murder but that she did have a pistol she wanted to dispose of. Two members of New York's Finest obligingly came to her door and took the Luger away.

While I was living in Omy's apartment I went to the Grand Concourse in the Bronx one night a week to meet a graduate student in the Classics who taught me ancient Greek grammar. I needed to learn Greek grammar, in order to major in the Classics when I returned to Princeton in the fall. The other evenings I was free to get together with friends, including Iurate Iasenas, my co-worker in the proofreading department. Iurate was a tall, beautiful blonde who lived in Queens. She invited me to come one night to meet her family and to see where she lived.

Before leaving Omy's apartment, as an afterthought, I called Iurate to be sure I had understood the directions to her house. Omy thought I had left. I heard waltz music coming from her bedroom and, while I was still talking on the phone, Omy came waltzing down the hall from the bedroom, doing turns to the music of Johann Strauss. She did a final one-two-three into the living room, graceful and in time with the music. She was stark naked. Seeing me seated on the couch, phone in hand, she continued to dance and, without missing a beat, twirled her way back up the hallway to her bedroom. I finished my phone call and headed out the door.

At the time I was too focused on getting together with Iurate to think very much about Omy's nude waltz. But as I think of it now, decades later, I recognize how wonderful and very much in character it was. She was already over 80, but as she was getting ready to take a bath, the melody and rhythm of the waltz filled her body and soul and sent her down the hall to the living room. It was her home, she thought she was alone, and the music had moved her to action. Why not? Perhaps nude was best for the romance of Strauss and the memories that came with it. Equally in character was that she did not miss a beat when she saw me, but turned in time to the music and danced back up the hallway. Nothing fazed her. She was ever calm and always carried on.

I shared Omy's interest in autograph collecting, a hobby she had started in the 1880s. She gave me her collection, which included autographs of the presidents in office during her childhood—

Chester A. Arthur, Benjamin Harrison, and Grover Cleveland. Growing up in Washington in the 1880s and '90s in a well-connected family, autograph collecting had not been hard for Omy. She drew on her connections. When I became interested in autograph collecting, Omy prevailed on her sister Jeanne to send her a 1952 letter Jeanne had received from her old friend Mamie Eisenhower after Ike's election. Omy wanted to give it to me for my collection.

In the 1880s Omy's family knew everyone in Washington, a much smaller town than it is today. Her paternal grandfather, William Maxwell Wood, had been a doctor in the navy. He was Fleet Surgeon of the Pacific Fleet before the Civil War, Fleet Surgeon of the Atlantic Fleet during the Civil War, and the US Navy's first Surgeon General after the Civil War. His career as a navy doctor gave him a ringside view of the battle between the ironclads *Monitor* and *Merrimack*. His career in the Pacific before the Civil War gave him the raw material to write successful books about the Far East. His writing paid for Rosewood Glen, the farm in Owing's Mills, Maryland, where he retired. Omy's father and Jennie Belle brought Omy and Jeanne to Rosewood Glen when they were toddlers.

Omy's maternal grandfather, Joseph Rodman West, was also a well-connected Washington figure. He had been a Union army general in the Civil War, a US Senator from Louisiana during Reconstruction, and then chief district commissioner in Washington. When Omy and her sister were children, they often visited the house on DuPont Circle, where Senator West and Jeanne Josephine lived. One side of their dining room was a floor-to-ceiling cage filled with beautiful, exotic birds.

Omy's father, William M. Wood, Jr., had also made a name for himself. After graduating from Annapolis, he developed a reputation as an inventor, doing pioneering work in refrigeration and winning a prize at the London Exposition for inventing an apparatus to lower lifeboats from the side of a ship.

Last but not least, Omy's Uncle Ern—C.E.S. Wood, a poet— knew everyone in the world of art and literature and produced Mark Twain's autograph for Omy's collection.

While Omy's well-connected family were not the French pirates Gramps joked about, they were a mix of strength and weakness, good and evil, and reflected the best and worst of 19th-century America. According to Uncle Ern, his father, the US Navy's first Surgeon General and successful author, was not quite all that his portrait in the dark blue dress uniform with gold buttons and braided epaulets suggested. No, according to Uncle Ern his father was a heavy drinker, opium addict, and at times, abusive husband.

Omy's maternal grandfather also hid a darker reality behind the public persona. In a photograph taken in Mathew Brady's studio, Joseph Rodman West looks very much the Reconstruction Senator: bald and bearded, he sports a three-quarter-length coat with velvet collar and wide lapels, spectacles hang on a chain over his brocade vest, and he wears a flamboyant silk tie. Omy may not have known it, but as a Union General in the Southwest during the Civil War, her grandfather gave the order to torture and kill the Apache leader, Mangas Coloradas, father-in-law of the great Apache warrior Cochise. By ordering the torture and murder of Mangas Coloradas, Joseph Rodman West prolonged the Indian Wars and earned the undying distrust of the Apache tribes for the US government.

This dark side of the family legacy was redeemed in part by Omy's colorful Uncle Ern, a West Pointer who also saw action during the Indian Wars, and who established a life-long friend-ship with Chief Joseph of the Nez Perce. Uncle Ern resigned his commission, graduated from Columbia Law School, and moved to Portland, Oregon, where he divided his time between commercial work and radical causes. He considered himself a "philosophical anarchist," not a bomb-thrower—although he defended some of the bomb-throwers, like Emma Goldman who plotted to kill robber baron Henry Clay Frick. Uncle Ern was a crusader for social justice, a published poet and political satirist who devoted his life to poetry and social causes from his California ranch, where he defiantly kept a vineyard to make wine during Prohibition.

After I returned to law school, Omy took several falls in her apartment on 82nd Street. Mom and Pop hired a housekeeper to limit her risk of falling and to keep an eye on her. But Omy did not like anyone keeping an eye on her and quickly fired the housekeeper. Mom and Pop hired another housekeeper. The pattern of hiring and firing repeated itself several times. Eventually, Mom persuaded Omy to come and live with them in the Big House. She moved into the guest room with the upstairs porch that she and Gramps had shared when they had come to visit. Her bedroom furniture was moved from her apartment into the guest room; it included the desk that Gramps had made for her and on which she wrote an endless stream of letters to her sister Jeanne and other relatives.

In 1968, the year after I graduated from law school, my college roommate, Win, married Mary in Cold Spring Harbor. All of our Princeton roommates gathered for the occasion—coming from North Carolina, Florida, and Pennsylvania—and filled all of the guest rooms in the Big House. One friend, Roger, had married a teetotaling Baptist, and had given up drinking. He flew from Florida to New York for the wedding but was a nervous flyer and decided to have just one drink to relax on the plane.

After the wedding, Roger and the rest of us sat by the pool on the lawn where the sheep had grazed during the Second World War. Sitting there together we had a bull session late into the night, telling tales of our lives both at and after Princeton. The storytelling was fueled by nightcaps, which ended up getting the better of all of us, but especially Roger.

The worse for wear, we all wandered upstairs to bed. In the second-floor hall, Roger made a left turn one door too early and passed out on the twin bed next to the bed in which Omy was sleeping. She woke as daylight was breaking and saw Roger's hand hanging over the side of the bed. She studied it and went back to sleep. When she woke again, Roger was gone. Omy walked down the hall to Mom's room to let her know, "Marion, there was a man in my room last night." She told Mom about her examination of the hand at the end of the arm that hung almost to the floor. "I knew that I was safe. It was a gentleman's hand," she explained. No reason for alarm or even to lose sleep. In Omy's frame of reference, the presence of a strange man in her bedroom did not rate as even the most trivial earthquake or slight tremor.

Omy died in early fall, the following year. Once, before she died, when I walked down the hallway past her room, she was talking in her sleep. She was having a conversation with her father, on the deck of a ship during a storm. True to form, she expressed no concern about the storm, but asked when the ship would come into port. The ship at last did find a far-away port and Omy's life ended. Until then, nothing could stop her, not the disfiguring tropical disease that ravaged her face, not the earthquakes that shook her home in Manila, not finding me unexpectedly on her couch as she waltzed naked into the room, nor waking up in Glen Cove to find my drunk Princeton roommate passed out on the bed next to hers, not the untimely death of her father a year before her wedding, not the death of Jeanne's infant baby a year after the wedding, and not even the hardest blow of all, the death of her own daughter, Jean, in 1933.

To Gramps and their friends, Omy was "Rose." Her name fit the beautiful, unstoppable woman with auburn hair who carried pink roses at her wedding.

CHAPTER 12.

My .300 H&H Magnum
(1963)

> How many young Heirs in England have
> gallop'd through their estates before they have
> been thirty?
>
> The Worth Of A Penny, *Dedication*

ON THE FLYLEAF of *Select Discourses* William Stoughton carefully noted Henry Peacham's observation that one of the ways young heirs "gallop'd" through their estates was by spending money "upon Drink and Women; for Bacchus and Venus are inseparable companions." In 1963, during my junior year at single-sex Princeton, Bacchus was a lot easier to find than Venus.

Perhaps in reaction to Princeton's barren environment, I chose to research and write my thesis on a book about love by a 12th-century French monk, Andreas Capellanus. Capellanus's *De Amore*, sometimes referred to as *The Art of Courtly Love*, at one level explicitly examines physical passion. Other levels of secular and religious meaning are less clear and have been much debated. After discussion with my faculty adviser, the analysis in my thesis would focus on religious allegory in *De Amore*. The project required studying the writings of the great figures of the medieval Church—such as Saint Augustine—in the original Latin. It was my goal for June and July 1963, to make real headway on this project, and I pored over

De Amore and the writings of medieval saints. I had studied Latin every year since the fifth grade and that summer I was at the peak of my reading comprehension skills—with the relatively modern sentence structure of medieval Latin, I could cover 40 or 50 pages an hour.

Each day I also spent a half hour or so with my .300 H&H Magnum, a serious long-range hunting rifle. It was a bolt-action Model 70 Winchester. There was nothing automatic about it. To load a shell, you raised the bolt handle on the right side of the rifle, sliding it backward and then forward again to load a shell into the chamber from a small metal clip in the wooden stock beneath the bolt. Firing it produced brutal recoil, hammering your shoulder. I had bought it for my planned August '63 trip to hunt wild Dall sheep in the Wrangell Mountains near Alaska's border with the Canadian Yukon. Alaska had not long been a state and oil would not be discovered at Prudhoe Bay for another four years. It was still a very wild place.

Glen Cove was not so wild. Even in 1963 you could not lawfully discharge a firearm within the city limits and I had no need or desire to punish my shoulder by actually shooting my rifle there. My daily practice was like the routine of a young archer in Sherwood Forest, holding a long bow at full draw to build up strength and steadiness for accurate shooting. In this form of training, the bowstring is never released and the arrow never flies. The analogy with a rifle is learning to hold it steady and to control your breathing so that you can pull the trigger without jarring the rifle and throwing off the shot. In between reading Saint Augustine and other works of medieval theology, I stood in my mental Sherwood Forest on the lawn behind the Big House and shouldered my unloaded .300 H&H Magnum. I practiced steadiness and breathing for "off-hand" shots while standing, and for more measured shots while seated and prone.

Hunting is atavistic—a call that lures the inner hunter-gatherer to bring game to the paleolithic fire or modern stove. There is something mystical in nature's call to the hunter, a unity between the hunter and the hunted. Charcoal and ochre paintings of bison, deer, and horses from thousands of years ago are in the caves of this hunter's soul. In more immediate terms, I inherited a love for both the outdoors and hunting from the father that I did not see enough, just as Gramps inherited his love of horses from the father who abandoned him. For good measure, whenever I go on a hunting trip—as I do every year with my son—I take along my grandfather's World War I sewing kit.

These days I hunt nothing larger than grouse and my favorite hunting gun is an old muzzleloader made in downtown Manhattan in the 1850s. The days of my .300 H&H Magnum and big-game hunting are long gone. Instead, for many years the most precious moments have been enjoying the hunt with enthusiastic dogs, an old gun, my son, and friends. My most recent memory is of a cool sunny afternoon spent on a farm on the Delaware River with my son and grandson, Will. We walked out of the field, my son carrying a side-by-side from the 1920s, me carrying a hammergun from the 1860s, and Will (without a gun at age seven) carrying a partridge. Will had enjoyed the day without firing a shot and, filling his grandfather's heart with joy, later that evening told his younger sister, Charlotta, that it was "the best day of my whole life."

Pop, who taught Sam and me how to shoot a .22 rifle safely, also did his best to teach us the worth of a penny. Critical to paying for my trip to Alaska in 1963 were savings bonds, which Pop had given me as a life lesson. I could sell the bonds and spend the money on whatever I wanted. Pop said, "You will learn that when you have spent the money, it is gone." That was fine with me. I was nowhere near 30, but like Peacham's young heirs, I had already "gallop'd" through part of my savings bonds buying first a FIAT 500 and then a VW Beetle. I would use what was left to fund a trip to the Yukon border and the most challenging hunt in the wildest place in the United States.

In the words of André Gide, I was determined to "turn my father's gold into dreams." Thinking back on it from a distance of more than half a century, I see that I may have turned my father's gold into a dream of my father. Perhaps I wanted to save the quiet and depressed man with the involuntary tics and shakes, to resurrect him in myself as the romantic figure who hunted marauding man-eaters near Saigon and dropped proposals to Mom from a plane.

But I had no such thoughts when I got on the plane to Anchorage with my .300 H&H Magnum. A few months later, when President Kennedy was killed in Dallas with a high-powered rifle, the world changed forever, but in early August 1963, I walked onto the plane at Idlewild International Airport (soon re-named John F. Kennedy International Airport) and handed my gun in its soft case to the flight attendant. "Where is a good place to stow my hunting rifle for the flight?"

"I can take care of it," she said. "We have a closet that is long enough." I don't remember whether my ammunition was in my carry-on or checked bags. I don't know that it mattered.

I was to be joined on the hunt by my friend, Cyr, but was traveling west alone—Cyr was first visiting his girlfriend (soon to be wife) in San Francisco. Not wanting to wait around I decided to go on ahead and fly into the area where we would hunt. I would use the time to get into shape, shoot some targets, and do some serious hiking. I checked my plan with Larry Folger, the outfitter in Chisana (pronounced "Shooshannah"), 50 miles from the nearest road in the wilderness of the Wrangell Mountains. Folger provided guides, saddle horses, packhorses, and food for $125 per day. He said it was OK for me to come early and do some hiking. I later learned from his hired man that my early arrival had made Folger suspect that I was an undercover agent from the Alaska Game Commission out to get him for a violation of the game laws.

Oblivious to Folger's suspicions, I flew in a DC-3 from Anchorage to Nabesna and then in a single engine Cessna to Chisana, landing among small saplings on a narrow strip 10 days before Cyr and I were scheduled to start our hunt.

When I arrived in Chisana the atmosphere was tense. A policeman had flown in just ahead of me because, I was told, Larry Folger and his neighbor were on the verge of killing each other. Folger, his wife or girlfriend, and a hired man, Jay, lived in one camp in Chisana, within spitting distance of the only other family within 50 miles of Chisana in any direction. Both Folger and his neighbor made a living providing guides, horses, and provisions to hunters with permits for Dall sheep, grizzlies, moose, or caribou. Folger's neighbor was married to a native Alaskan, an Aleut. They had two beautiful daughters. But Folger, hotheaded and a bigot, dismissed the children as "half-breeds." He and his neighbor hated each other.

I quickly got to know Jay, Folger's hired man, who told me that Folger had recently hidden in a mountain pass, through which he expected his neighbor to cross. Jay believed Folger's plan had been to shoot and kill his neighbor. Luckily the neighbor never arrived.

Nevertheless, someone in the microscopic community of Chisana was sufficiently concerned about Folger's threatening behavior to contact the police. The policeman did his best to defuse the situation and then left.

For the next 10 days, before Cyr joined me, I did some hiking, taking my rifle along because of possible encounters with moose and grizzlies. I got as far as Bonanza Creek, several hours away over mountain trails from Chisana. Bonanza Creek was the site of the last gold rush in Alaska in 1915. I spent time there panning and "sluicing" for gold with an 80-year-old hobby prospector who had worked for a supplier in the mining camp during the 1915 gold rush. After retiring he came back to Bonanza Creek from time to time to camp and pan for gold.

A huge cast-iron bathtub sat on the ground among the abandoned miners' cabins. It had once been inside the whorehouse next to the saloon. The old prospector said it had been carried over the mountains by four giant Swedes for the women of the whorehouse who serviced the miners and relieved them of their money. The old prospector said that not many of the miners left Bonanza Creek with any savings.

Folger's despised neighbor had a camp in one of the abandoned miner's cabins near Bonanza Creek. When I returned to Chisana from my hike, Jay told me that his counterpart, Jackson, who worked for the neighbor, had stolen Jay's rifle clip and ammunition and taken them to Bonanza Creek. It may have been true, but it may also have been a story fabricated by Folger, who saw conspiracies everywhere. After my return to New York from Alaska, Jay told me that Folger became convinced that Jay was conspiring against him. Indeed, Jay eventually left Chisana after Folger came up behind him and hit him in the back with a two-by-four, injuring him, but fortunately not killing him.

12. My .300 Magnum (1963)

In any event, in August 1963, Jay believed that Jackson had stolen his rifle clip and ammunition and asked if I would go with him to Bonanza Creek to get his property back. I would have to bring my .300 H&H Magnum along, since Jay no longer had a clip or ammunition for his rifle. To achieve the element of surprise, we would do the hike at night, so we could "jump" Jackson in his cabin before he woke up in the morning. Being young and booksmart but not remotely lifesmart, I agreed.

Jay and I woke ourselves up in the middle of the night. We were in the land of the midnight sun and the hike to Bonanza Creek was done in twilight. We passed within 200 yards of a shadowy moose in a creek bottom. On the opposite side of the valley from the trail we watched a grizzly effortlessly power up a steep slope in a matter of seconds in a breathtaking display of the bear's strength and speed.

We reached Bonanza Creek before anyone was awake. Jay knew which cabin Jackson was in. We silently approached. I had my rifle ready. We threw open the door and rushed in. On his cot, Jackson sat bolt upright in terror.

Jay said, "Give me the fucking rifle clip. Give me the ammunition."

"What the fuck are you talking about?" Jackson replied. "I have no idea where your rifle clip is or where your ammunition is." His face showed disbelief that we should be standing in front of him making this accusation. In an instant everything changed. Jay and I looked at each other. We believed the terrified Jackson. We talked for a while with him and apologized while my rifle leaned against the wall in a corner of the cabin. When we got back to Chisana, Jay found his rifle clip and ammunition on a chair under some dirty laundry near his bunk.

Thinking about that pre-dawn raid of Jackson's cabin, I know that the split seconds after Jay and I burst through the cabin door could have led to a very different outcome. Jay or I, or both of us could have been dead the instant we opened the door. Jackson could have been injured or killed. I could have spent years, if not a lifetime, in prison in Alaska. Instead of turning my father's gold into dreams, I could have turned my father's dreams into tears.

As fortune had it, Jay, Jackson, and I were unharmed. A day or so later Cyr arrived. We hunted for three weeks and were fogged in at Chisana for another week before a bush plane could fly in to take us to Anchorage. We were a week behind schedule. For all Mom and Pop knew, we were lost in the mountains or worse. I called them from Anchorage to let them know we were OK and then, in the Anchorage motel where we spent the night before leaving, Cyr and I—in turn after turn—took multiple showers to cleanse us of the month spent in the wilderness with neither bath nor shower. We flew out of Anchorage the next day.

Mom and Pop picked me up at Idlewild. They were glad to see me, despite the beard. We hugged. I told them tales of my adventures but I did not say a word about the raid at Bonanza Creek.

Once again the evil spirits from Stoughton's flyleaf notes had looked the other way. In my life I have done many dumb things, but Bonanza Creek was possibly the dumbest. No one was hurt and I was able to go back to New York, meet my future wife, and go to law school.

The year I went to Alaska, Joan Baez wrote a song called "There but for fortune":

Show me the prison, show me the jail,
Show me the prisoner whose life has gone stale
And I'll show you a young man with so many reasons why
And there but for fortune, go you or I.

I think of that song and of the stupid things I have survived because Stoughton's evil spirits gave me a pass. Luck has smiled on me more often than I give her credit for, and since Bonanza Creek, I have been a true believer that "there but for fortune, go you or I."

CHAPTER 13.

Adventure with the Jack of All Trades
(1971)

Some men are thrifty and sparing by nature;
yea, saving even in trifles.

The Worth Of A Penny, *p. 20*

L<small>IKE</small> S<small>TOUGHTON</small> and his thrifty prophet, Henry Peacham, my brother Tom believed in frugality: While in the army on a US rocket base in Thrace, northwest of Istanbul, he re-sharpened his razor blades rather than spend money on new ones.

Stoughton's flyleaf notes record another of Henry Peacham's themes: the need to be open to any occupation that necessity requires. "Think no Labour Slavery That brings in Penny Savery" (a "savery" being a small meat pie). Stoughton's notes also reference Peacham's cautionary tale of three soldiers condemned to be hanged for their crimes. The soldiers were told they would be spared the noose if they agreed to go to work for either a bricklayer, a brewer, or a farmer of hops. Two of the condemned men immediately agreed to work for the bricklayer and the brewer. The third, a picky and snooty Englishman, was offered the chance to work for the farmer. He refused. He was not, he said, brought up "to gather Hops, but desired to be hanged first," and, as the story concludes, "so he was."

To survive, Peacham's soldiers had to be open to different,

possibly unfamiliar, employment. My ex-soldier brother took this philosophy to heart and pursued many lines of work during decades spent in the Middle East following his time in the army. He was a journalist, an aircraft mechanic, a shipper of fruits and vegetables, and a historian in search of clues from the upper Tigris and Euphrates as to where on Mount Ararat Noah's ark found dry land after the flood. In Tom's day, as now, Mount Ararat was located in the Kurdish area of eastern Turkey.

In 1964, when Michelle and I were married in Brussels, Tom told me he was exporting melons from the Middle East to Scandinavia. Lending some credence to the story, he showed up in Belgium in a beaten-up old Mercedes with two very attractive Danish girls who allegedly played some role in the Scandinavian end of his melon exporting business.

But Tom was ever a mystery man. What line of work he would pursue next was anybody's guess. Mom said we could always look forward to the next incarnation.

In July 1971 Tom was living in Beirut and I was a mid-level associate at Milbank Tweed Hadley & McCloy working on corporate transactions, securities, and ship and aircraft financing. The people at Milbank were wonderful, but my work at the firm was dull beyond my wildest dreams.

We were a few weeks away from Michelle's due date with Scott, our second child. No one in the family had heard from Tom in over a month when, just after the Fourth of July, Mom got a call from the State Department. Tom was in solitary confinement in a military prison in Diyarbakir, Turkey. I later learned that he had been kept in a windowless cell under a floor on which Turkish soldiers marched back and forth, preventing him from sleeping. When they discovered he liked yoghurt, they stopped giving him yoghurt. After a month they let him make a call to the US

Consulate. None of the criminal defense lawyers in Diyarbakir wanted to defend him but, at last, a lawyer agreed to take the case and at least appear in the courtroom with Tom before he was, potentially, sentenced to death.

I had visited Tom in Turkey twice before—once with our parents in the late 1950s and once after my freshman year in college. Tom and I had traveled together from Istanbul inland into Asia Minor and then back up the coast—on one leg of the trip we hitchhiked on a sponge-fishing boat from Bodrum to Izmir. From Izmir we moved on to Istanbul and from there we swam across the Bosporus from Asia to Europe. Our Turkish friend, Erol, rowed alongside us to keep an eye out for tanker traffic and other hazards, ready to pull us into the boat in an emergency. Erol's friend Miné swam with us. She was six inches shorter than me and eight inches shorter than Tom. We all made it, but Miné reached the shore of Europe first.

In spite of these previous visits, I had no idea where Diyarbakir was until I checked the atlas before flying to Turkey for Tom's trial. The city was the provincial capital of a remote Kurdish region of eastern Turkey—because of Kurdish dissident activity, the area was under Turkish military rule.

The US State Department said that Tom was to be tried in a military court in Diyarbakir for treason and attempting to overthrow the Turkish government—crimes punishable by death. Drayton Middleton, the man from the State Department who contacted Mom with the news, told her that he believed it could help Tom to have a family member present at the trial. Mom called me and gave me Middleton's number.

I sat at my desk and dialed. Middleton picked up. By way of background, he told me that the military judges who would decide Tom's fate were Turkish Army Colonels, some, or all, of whom came from the border region in eastern Turkey. He came quickly to the point: the presence of a family member during the trial would generate sympathy for Tom. In the local culture, the presence of a relative, a brother in particular, would be important.

"Can you go?" Middleton asked.

"Yes."

"You have to be in Diyarbakir in two days. Call me with your flight information. The consul from Adana will meet you at the Diyarbakir airport."

Middleton also explained some rules of decorum I should follow in the courtroom in Diyarbakir:

"Don't cross your legs so that you show the soles of your shoes to the judges. That's an unforgivable sign of disrespect."

I don't remember exactly what I told my colleagues at Milbank or the details of my conversation with Michelle, but the following day I headed to JFK Airport. Before leaving I had spent some time in the United Nations Library reading English language versions of the death-penalty statutes under which Tom was being tried. I also read the Turkish Constitution, which on the surface had many similarities to the US Constitution. Armed with that information and Middleton's advice I was as well prepared as I was going to be. I went home, packed, went to JFK, and lined up at the counter to check my bag and show my tourist-class ticket.

The airline representative said, "I'll reissue your ticket. You are first class to Rome."

"There must be a mistake," I said. The whole family, including Mom, had inherited some Puritan frugality. We did not travel anywhere first class.

"You've been switched to first class," the clerk repeated. "Somebody must like you."

I slept in luxury on the flight to Rome, then made the connecting flight to Istanbul. I was in the Istanbul Airport long enough to buy a souvenir Meerschaum pipe before the flight to Diyarbakir.

In Diyarbakir, I walked down the ramp into 110-degree heat. The consul met me at the bottom of the ramp with his assistant. We dropped off my bag at the hotel and headed for the military base, where the trial had already started.

On the way, the consul told me that the main evidence against Tom was that he had been arrested with a Kurdish–Turkish dictionary in his VW Beetle as he crossed eastern Turkey on his way from Beirut, where he was living, to Istanbul. Diyarbakir was under military rule and did not welcome tourists. He was stopped, and when the dictionary was found in his car, he was charged with treason and attempting to overthrow the government.

The consul explained that the trial had recessed following a discussion between Tom's attorney and the Colonels as to whether, as a matter of law, possession of the dictionary alone was sufficient to support Tom's conviction. Before I walked into the courtroom and sat down with the soles of my shoes pressed firmly to the floor, the Colonels had asked for an advisory opinion from the faculty of the Law School in Ankara. The Colonels were awaiting the opinion. Tom was not present in the courtroom.

The opinion came within an hour or two of my arrival. The faculty opined that possession of the dictionary was insufficient evidence for a conviction. One of the Colonels, who appeared to be the chief judge, gestured for the consul and me to join him at the side of the courtroom. We were ushered into a small room. Tom was brought into the room through a side door. My brother was wide-eyed, either from sleeplessness or stress, or surprise both at his acquittal and at seeing me. We had no time to speak.

The judge turned to me and asked, "What do you think of our system of justice?"

I said, "It is admirable. The Turkish Constitution is very similar to the United States Constitution."

Pleasantries over, the judge said that Tom would be "released" to the Diyarbakir police who would take us to the parking lot where his car was being stored. Tom would be expelled from Turkey and was not welcome to return. A local policeman would go with us to the Syrian border to ensure that we did, indeed, leave the country. We were directed to an open-top police Jeep. In the expectation that the local police would take us directly to Tom's car, the consul and his driver left for the hotel, so that they could get to the airport in time for the flight to Adana.

Tom and I found ourselves in the back of the Jeep behind two policemen headed, or so we thought, to the parking lot and Tom's car. It did not happen. Instead, the policemen drove us through the hot, dusty streets reaching neither a parking lot nor a garage. We came to the outskirts of town. A boy on a tractor backed into the road in front of us, to the annoyance of the policemen; the driver slammed on the brakes. The other officer jumped out, grabbed the boy, and threw him onto the floor of the Jeep, apparently intending to deal with him later.

After another 10 minutes of driving, we stopped at a police station. One of the policemen took the boy inside and returned. We drove on, stopping at another police station. Tom and I were told to wait in the Jeep, while the two policemen disappeared into the building. We had no idea where we were, and still expecting to be taken to Tom's car, we stayed in the Jeep.

After 10 or 15 minutes the policemen returned and drove us to a square with a fountain. There were shade trees and tables and chairs where the public could sit and escape the stifling Diyarbakir heat. Again we were told to wait. Again we did as we were told—surely the VW was nearby.

Once more the policemen reappeared and drove us to another police station. This time Tom and I were ushered through the massive front door into the building. Inside, we stood in a small lobby with the two policemen. Suddenly, they grabbed Tom by the arms and pushed him through a door on the far side of the lobby. The door slammed shut. I was alone in the lobby.

Just waiting there seemed like a bad option. Instead, I opened the heavy front door onto the street and started to run. We had driven from place to place in an unfamiliar Turkish city and I had no idea where I was. I ran, looking for traffic and a taxi. Within a few blocks, I found a cab. I gave the driver the name of the hotel where I had a room and where I hoped to find the consul. My luck was out, the desk clerk spoke enough English to give me the bad news. "I am sorry, they left for the airport some time ago."

I bolted from the lobby onto the street and into another taxi. "Airport, please."

At the airport, I crossed the runway behind the small, provincial terminal building and saw the consul and his assistant climbing the ramp up to the plane to Adana. I ran to the side of the ramp. Sweating and winded, I gasped out the words, "The police kidnapped my brother."

The two men came down off the ramp. As we headed to the street I explained what had happened. The consul hailed a cab and we headed to the provincial Governor's Mansion, where the consul demanded an emergency meeting with the governor. We sat in the governor's office and the consul repeated the facts of Tom's acquittal, how we had subsequently been taken from place to place, and how Tom had been kidnapped. At first, the governor disclaimed knowledge about "any of this." But the consul persisted and said that unless he wanted an international incident, the governor must direct the police to release my brother and produce his car so that he could leave the country. The governor was silent.

I was too young and stupid to keep my mouth shut. Having read the Turkish Constitution in the UN Library, I said to the governor, "My brother was acquitted. The police are violating the Turkish Constitution." The governor glared at me. He dismissed my ignorant opinion, responding in heavily accented English, "The Turkish Constitution only applies to innocent people."

The consul repeated the possibility of an international incident between NATO allies.

At last the governor made a call to the city's police headquarters. The consul, his assistant, and I were taken to the police station where Tom was held, and Tom's car was produced. This time, it was agreed between the consul and the police that the consul's assistant would stay with us until we crossed into Syria.

Once more the consul headed for the airport. Tom, the assistant, one of the Diyarbakir policemen, and I got into the VW and headed for Syria. Tom drove, the assistant sat beside him, I sat behind the assistant, and the policeman sat behind Tom. For the entire drive the policeman sat with a pistol in his lap. I can't now recall how long it took us to reach the Syrian border but I do know that I didn't take my eyes off that gun for a second.

When we arrived, the Turkish-Syrian border crossing was closed for the day. We had to stay in a dingy hotel on the Turkish side. The policeman booked two rooms. He made it clear that the assistant and I would stay in one room while he, his revolver, and Tom would stay in the other. We argued. The policeman said that he had to stay in the same room as Tom. In that case, we said, we would all spend the night together in one room.

We did not sleep. Tom, the assistant, and I stayed up watching the policeman and his gun all night. We reached the Syrian border as soon as it opened after dawn. Somehow, the Syrian border guards knew that an American was being expelled from Turkey. They thought it was very funny. One of the guards had a spear, which he banged on a shield, dancing and laughing in celebration at the sight of Americans in this predicament. Tom and I drove into Syria with the border guards celebrating in the rear-view mirror. The policeman and the consul's assistant stayed in Turkey.

The dancing border guard did not bode well. Hafez al-Assad had just consolidated his power in Syria in a final military coup. Kurds were Syria's largest ethnic minority and Kurdish separatists were a perennial thorn in the side of the Syrian government. Assad's security forces might be interested in an American expelled from Turkey after being arrested in the Kurdish border region in possession of a Kurdish–Turkish dictionary.

We took turns driving. Tom was at the wheel when we crossed into Syria. Once we were out of sight of the crossing, he accelerated. He drove the Beetle as fast as it could go towards Aleppo and south towards Hama and then the Lebanese border.

At first, the landscape was vast and empty, crossed by rough roads, sometimes paved, sometimes dirt, not yet improved by Assad's highway-building program. Neither of us had had enough sleep. Indeed, it had been a long time since Tom had had a restful night. He asked me to take over the driving.

As we approached a village, beggars swarmed into the street in front of the car. I slowed down.

Tom said, "Speed up! Step on the gas!" I did as he said. The beggars, many of them children, parted like the Red Sea before Moses and the VW sped through the village into the empty landscape beyond.

By nightfall, we had reached Hama, a city on the banks of the Orontes River in central Syria, where a decade later Assad's forces would slaughter thousands of dissidents and bulldoze sections of the city. In mid July 1971, Hama was peaceful. We had dinner on a terrace overlooking the Orontes—grilled lamb and an eggplant dish, a glass of red wine, bread, and an unidentifiable dip. It all tasted good. The night was cool. At last, I thought, we must be out of the woods. Exhausted, we walked back to the hotel and turned in for the night.

The moonlit dinner had been an illusion of peace and safety. Tom woke me up at 2:00 in the morning. He may have sensed that we were not safe in Syria. As in Turkey, Kurdish separatism was a major concern in Syria and if the Syrian government learned that Tom had been tried in Turkey for conspiring with Kurdish rebels, tarrying in Syria presented risks. Tom wanted to keep moving. It was pitch black outside our windows. He woke me and said, "We're leaving." Back in the car Tom was loud and clear, "Step on the gas! Don't slow down!" Just as before, I obeyed my older brother. We continued south past the medieval castle at Masyaf, where Shia Muslim warriors known as the "Assassins" held off both Crusaders and the army of Sunni Sultan Saladin.

We crossed into Lebanon and sped on to Beirut and Tom's apartment.

I was to spend the night in the apartment, which he shared with his German girlfriend, "Froggie." We had not been there for two minutes before the fight began. Tom was in a rage: Why hadn't Froggie called the US Consul in Beirut when he didn't come home for weeks after he said he would be back? Froggie responded that she didn't make any calls because she was sure he was in Istanbul with his other girlfriend. The fight was loud and I was already getting sick from something I had eaten in the restaurant over-looking the Orontes.

The next day I left for New York, nauseated with dysentery taking over my body. I called home as soon as we landed. Michelle was about to deliver. I found a taxi and went straight to Columbia Presbyterian Hospital in Manhattan, arriving just in time to welcome the arrival of our son Scott. Not even dysentery could mar the beautiful ending to an insane few days.

Back in my office at Milbank, in between doctor's appointments, I opened my desk drawer. There was the yellow legal pad on which I had written Middleton's telephone number at the State Department. I paused, why not call him, thank him for his help, and make sure he knew that Tom was out of prison and safely in Beirut? I dialed the number.

"May I speak with Drayton Middleton, please?"

"I am sorry. Nobody by that name works here."

Perhaps I had mis-dialed.

"Is this the State Department?"

"Yes, sir."

"I was trying to call..." I read out the number on the paper, the number on which I had called and spoken to Middleton not that many days before, the number that Middleton had given Mom when the State Department had first contacted us.

"No, sir. Nobody by that name works here."

Almost 30 years later, on September 11, 2001, I walked home from my office in lower Manhattan across Broadway from the World Trade Center. Like countless others I had sheltered in a stairwell as the street was engulfed in the colossal black cloud that surged across Broadway, up Liberty Street, and onto Nassau Street. I stayed in the back entrance to 120 Broadway until the cloud lifted enough to breathe and see, and then walked the nine miles home covered with dust from the pulverized Twin Towers. As I walked, I felt fear and a closeness to death that made me think of Tom.

When I was a little kid, my brother Tom seemed more like an uncle, breaking up fights between Sam and me. By the time I went away to boarding school and then college, Tom had been my partner in several experiences on or far over the edge of safety— driving in a Spanish racing car at high speeds on the back roads of Oyster Bay or gliding toward the Atlantic Ocean in late November on the way back to Long Island from Nantucket in Tom's old and barely operational single-engine plane, which sputtered and died in the sky as rust jammed the fuel line from the auxiliary fuel tank. After the engine died, the plane took a dive toward the ocean, began to sputter, re-started, climbed, and died again several times before the fuel line opened up once more. Instead of crashing and dying in the cold Atlantic we made it to Long Island and a bottle of bourbon on Crescent Beach Road.

After 9/11 I told Tom that I had felt close to death several times in my life and that the biggest difference between those earlier experiences and this was that on 9/11 he had not been with me.

CHAPTER 14.

Mom Talks about Things Like the Pillow Fight
(1989–2001)

Your mother is like a goddess who comes
down to visit with us mortals once in a while.

Dr. Stephen Marks, Mom's doctor, 1994

I T WAS the worst turbulence I have ever flown through. The big
Olympic Airways jet was heading east over the Balkans on the way
to Athens through a winter storm. The plane repeatedly dropped,
climbed, and lurched from side to side. Heavy rain pelted the fuse-
lage and bursts of lightning flashed over the mountains below. We
were on our way to spend Christmas in Cyprus with my brother,
Tom, and his family. Tom had been in Cyprus for nearly six years.
At the time of our visit in December 1989, Barbara and I had been
together for almost six months. From our seats on the plane we
had a good view of two flight attendants in the galley, a man and a
woman. Both were on the floor with their feet up, jammed against
the galley drawers to keep them from flying open and spilling food
and service trays onto the floor. The flight attendants repeatedly
crossed themselves. My teenagers, Sylvia and Scott, were sitting
behind us dressed in late '80s grunge. Barbara and I were holding
onto the armrests. Mom, 89, also seated behind us, showed no

concern whatsoever. She was dressed in a wool suit, white gloves, and a hat—Mom had high standards for everything, including what to wear on a plane.

We landed in Athens in the morning and took an uneventful connecting flight to Nicosia in better weather. Along the way we noticed that, very occasionally, Mom took a whiff of something in a small bottle from her purse.

"What is that, Mom?"

"Nothing really. Smelling salts. They help, if you feel a little faint."

"Have you talked with Doctor Marks about that?"

"Nothing to worry about."

Nothing to worry about was an irregular heartbeat, but Mom was determined to enjoy the trip. When we got back to New York after New Year's, Mom spoke with Dr. Marks and then with the cardiologist. She was given a pacemaker. She lived on for more than another 10 years, until February 2001, approaching her 101st birthday.

Mom's life spanned three centuries. She was born in the last year of the 19th century and lived into the first year of the 21st century. She was consistently stoic in the face of anything unpleasant or painful. When she had bad pains in her stomach in her 80s, she chose to ignore them. She gleefully told her friend Muriel that she had been suffering excruciating stomach pain, but that it had gone away. Thankfully, Muriel did not see this as a cause for glee and made Mom promise to visit Dr. Marks immediately. After diagnostic tests, Dr. Marks referred her to a surgeon for an emergency operation to remove a large pancreatic cyst. Mom was not given good odds on surviving the surgery, but she did. She even survived the surgeon and lived on for almost two more decades.

Despite whatever unpleasantness or pain life threw her way, Mom was determined to enjoy life—her friends, opera, cooking, travel, good conversation, politics, and baseball. She was a Mets fan.

After living as a single woman through the Roaring Twenties, pursued by many suitors both in and out of the military, Mom married Pop when she was 30. He was a staunch Republican for whom the mere mention of FDR's name during a meal was enough to make him leave the table. But marriage did not affect Mom's politics. The older she became, the more liberal she became. In the '90s Bill Clinton was her man. George W. Bush she considered a comedown. Growing up in the military, loyalty was as important to Mom as it was to a good soldier in battle—whatever bad news she heard about Bill Clinton, he was still her man.

Dr. Marks, her physician for more than 20 years, observed that Mom was distant, like a "goddess who comes down to visit with us mortals once in a while." She was, indeed, always a beautiful goddess. As Dr. Marks asked her in her 90s, "When are you going to get wrinkles?"

That image of the distant goddess was also seen and captured by the artist who did the portrait that hung over the mantel in the big room of the house in Glen Cove. In it her dark red velvet dress was warm, but she seemed severe, even cold, gazing into the distance.

In her life Mom experienced significant disappointments and losses—her younger sister, Jean, died in circumstances that left Mom with deep feelings of guilt; her marriage with Pop was far from any anticipated bed of roses; her first grandchild, Rosie, died young, even younger than Mom's sister. Being distant may have been Mom's way of dealing with the pain of life. But, despite it all, she was generous and sociable, enjoyed many friends, and was always a supportive mother.

I must admit, though, that growing up with Mom was no walk in the park. She was not particularly interested in children until they had something interesting to say. When Sam and I were little, she regularly had migraines. When she was having a migraine, it was especially important to respect her need for distance. I did not always understand this. When Mom was in her 40s and I was eight years old or younger, I could not get enough of her and wanted more attention than I got. Once, she was lying on her bed waiting for a painful migraine to go away. Miss Julie, one of our two miniature poodles, was lying next to her. I could not get Mom's attention and failing in that effort, I tried to get Miss Julie's attention instead. Miss Julie was not as good-natured as our male poodle, Domino. Miss Julie wanted no part of my attempt to play with her. When I patted her, she growled. Heard through a splitting headache, to Mom Miss Julie's soft growl may have sounded louder than it was. She told me to stop annoying Miss Julie. I did not want to annoy Miss Julie, I wanted to pat her. I wanted her attention. I patted Miss Julie again. It produced the same outcome—another low growl, which thundered inside Mom's head. I do not remember how many times I repeated this behavior before Mom said, "If you do that one more time, your father will give you a spanking." I did it one more time. When he got home, Pop came up to my room and gave me the only spanking I ever had in my life. I don't think it was something he enjoyed. When he was finished, he said, "My father used to take me down to the stable and spank me with a horsewhip."

I now recognize that there were good reasons for Mom's migraines. She had graduated 12th grade at Holton-Arms in Washington, DC, in 1918, and like most women of that era she did not go to college, let alone business school. Yet here she was, later in life, running a business. Nothing had gone as planned. In the late 1940s Pop had a stroke on the squash court. It left him paralyzed for months and he walked around the house on crutches. He also began to suffer from bouts of depression.

Pop pulled out of the plastics business in which he had lost hundreds of thousands of 1948 dollars and started a new business importing, distributing, and selling small foreign cars. In both businesses, Pop had had a vision—both visions were ahead of their time. The public appetite for wrapping, bagging, and boxing everything in plastic and for small foreign cars was just over the horizon. Brewster Automobiles, based in Oyster Bay, struggled to stay afloat just as Pop's own struggles with depression worsened.

Pop, "Chick" to Mom, was no longer the romantic figure she had married. He spent more and more time away in hospitals, "sanitariums," and on ranches in search of an elusive diagnosis and cure for his depression. He was given electric-shock therapy, relaxation therapy, and everything in between at various places between New England and Arizona. For extended periods, while he was away, Mom ran Brewster Automobiles.

When Pop was home, he and Mom had cocktails every evening in the library. They sat on the couch. Goldfish or Triscuits with smoked Vermont cheddar cheese were generally laid out in front of the couch on the round bronze Indian table with its engraved and painted scenes of life and wildlife in India. Sometimes Pop's jaw moved involuntarily. Sometimes he had the shakes. He used the cocktails as self-medication for both his depression and the shakes. He always had more than one martini before dinner (in addition to the martinis before lunch) and he smoked at least two packs of Lucky Strikes a day. The Luckies he smoked in the library ended up in a large amber-colored glass ashtray on the Indian table.

During cocktail hour, Mom did needlepoint—a skill she had learned from Omy. Over the years she created four rugs, each of six square panels with a border of narrower rectangular panels around the outside. The first of the rugs was made as a present for Pop. It showed the three tigers, the elephant, wild boar, and deer that he had hunted on his trip around the world after graduating from Princeton in 1923. The rug's border was a long chain of flowering vines through which monkeys climbed. Pop had also killed a peacock on the trip; a peacock was depicted in the bottom center panel. Mom said that Grandmother Brewster was horrified that Pop had killed a peacock. For Grandmother Brewster each of the bird's beautiful tail feathers displayed an evil eye. If you killed a peacock, those eyes would haunt you and bring bad luck. But not everyone shared her superstition. For others, the peacock and its beautiful feathers symbolized kindness, compassion, and eternal love. To me Grandmother Brewster's interpretation sounded right and went hand in hand with the "Evil Spirits" in the witchcraft judge's book.

In any case, that beautiful first rug was finally finished and went beneath the bronze Indian table in the library, where Pop could enjoy it, and perhaps remember the hunter of man-eaters and the dashing pilot he had once been.

After Gramps died and Sam was away at boarding school, Mom paid more attention to me. Most nights during the school week, she helped me with my French, Latin, and history homework. I went with her to the print shop where she was always on the lookout for an Audubon giant folio print to frame and hang in our house in Vermont. Mom loved Audubon's birds of prey and bought beautiful prints of eagles, falcons, and hawks for our vacation home.

I preferred the Audubon prints of furry animals that were in the folders at the Sea Cliff print shop. During one of our trips to the print shop, I spotted a six-by-ten-inch Audubon print that meant more to me than any of the eagles, hawks, and falcons. It showed a log with two very small skunks in a hollow and a protective, snarling mother skunk on top of the log. I liked the idea of the mother skunk guarding the two little stinkers, protecting them from any harm. I saw Sam and me in that hollow log. Mom bought the small print for me and had it framed so I could hang it on the wall of my room. I believe that, just as I always craved Mom's attention, I wanted to feel safe like the small skunks, protected from the evil spirits that haunted the family, gave Pop the shakes, and led Uncle Sydney to murder and suicide.

There is no snug hollow in life that guarantees safety and sanctuary or ensures an ideal existence. For 18 years my married life with Michelle was in many ways charmed and idyllic—we had two wonderful children, a brownstone next to Prospect Park in Brooklyn, and a farm in Pennsylvania a mile down the road from Sam's farm. Charmed or not, my marriage fell apart. I had an affair with Mary, a fellow member of the Board of Trustees at Sylvia and Scott's school in Park Slope, who was recently divorced from her husband. I moved in to Mary's house. No amount of marriage counseling and therapy could repair my marriage. Like Humpty Dumpty, "all the King's horses and all the King's men" could not put it back together again, and I refused to try. For me the love was gone. Michelle filed for divorce. I was served with a summons in the reception area of the Manhattan law firm where I was a partner. Acrimonious and expensive litigation followed to the enrichment of two divorce lawyers hired by Michelle and one hired by me. After five painful years, the divorce became final. My relationship with Mary did not survive and I moved into my own apartment in Brooklyn.

However sad Mom was about my divorce, she was always supportive, always loyal. As the years went by I spent more time with her both on my own and then together with Barbara, before and after Barbara and I married. At some point the subject of extra-marital affairs came up in a conversation. I don't remember whether the trigger was Bill Clinton's relationship with Monica Lewinsky, my relationship with Mary, or the wild antics of people Mom and Pop knew on Long Island in the Roaring Twenties and beyond.

What Mom said, rather than the particular context of her words, struck me: "I never had an affair with anyone in your father's social class." Mom was not class conscious and her comment was not striking because she used the term "class." What was striking was the unspoken negative. If she chose to say "I never had an affair with anyone in your father's social class," she left open the pos-sibility that she had had an affair with someone outside of Pop's "social class." She volunteered no more information and, instead, flew back to her distant perch. She had given as much as she chose to give and that was that. I do not know if she intended to dis-close that she had had an affair with someone. I do not know if she wanted me to ask. Nor do I know, had I asked, if she would have revealed a long-kept secret or just moved farther away into the distance. In any case, out of habit, I did not press her. She con-trolled the distance and I respected it.

I did not jump to any conclusions. Pop had been in the throes of depression leading to hospitals, therapies, and long stays away from home. Through it all, I never heard Mom complain, but her life must have been difficult, painful, and lonely. That comment, so many years later, made me think of something that had happened during those hard times when Pop was away and she was running the business.

Then a teenager, I was coming up the stone steps to the end of the back terrace of the Big House. Both the steps and I were hidden by a hedge. I could hear our movie-star-handsome gardener,

Peter, and Mom having a conversation. They were on the other side of the hedge, at the end of the terrace above the orchard far from the main living areas of the house and away from the part of the terrace we typically used. Peter was crying, saying, "I can't stand it anymore." The conversation was clearly private, not meant to be overheard, so I backed down the steps, entered the house through the basement door, walked past Peter's tool room and the wine cellar, and up the stairs to the kitchen. Consciously, I made nothing—or avoided making anything—of what I had overheard. My subconscious made more of it. I had always liked Peter, but after hearing that snippet of conversation, I had a recurring dream of Oedipal rage in which I murdered Peter in the wine cellar—I came up behind him with a screwdriver and stabbed him to death.

Peter and his family soon moved out of the East Cottage and, with financial help from Pop, bought or built a home in Oyster Bay. Peter's brother, Robert, replaced him as our gardener. But Robert and his family never moved into the East Cottage, instead, he came to the Big House by the day to do the gardening and mowing. I do not remember much about Robert, except that he had his brother's movie-star looks. Once I heard Mom yell at him out of a second-floor window to put his shirt on while he was working.

After that, sometime in the late 1950s, Pop got back into sailing. The automobile business and the trips back and forth to hospitals were in the past, although Pop still self-medicated with martinis and Lucky Strikes. Overall, though, Mom and Pop's life seemed better. They spoke about their happy days sailing his weekender sloop, *Blue Sky*, in the years after they were first married. Now Pop had the Knudsen Boat Yard in Huntington build *Rose Wood*— similar in size to *Blue Sky*, except with a yawl rig. The divided sail plan made the boat easier to handle. Pop and Mom sailed *Rose Wood* for the last 10 years of his life.

Not only did Pop name the boat after Omy, his mother-in-law, but he named *Rose Wood*'s dinghy *Rose Maxwell* after my sister Isabel's daughter, my niece Rosie. Rosie was Mom's first grandchild and Omy's namesake. She was a beautiful, talented child who grew into a lovely young woman, a bright star in everyone's universe for as long as she lived. Rosie's death at age 22 and its devastating effect on Isabel were heavy blows for Mom. When she heard the news, she cried for both her granddaughter and daughter—it was the only time I remember Mom crying since Dimitri and I broke the Lalique birds.

After Rosie's death in 1983 and my divorce from Michelle four years later, I spent much less time at my farm in Pennsylvania. As long as Mom lived in the Big House, Barbara and I visited her there for holidays and in between. We often watched *In Julia's Kitchen* together. Mom made the best corn pudding and Yorkshire pudding on the planet. Inspired by the time she, Pop, and I had spent in France in 1958, she also did *oeufs-en-gelée*, dishes with homemade mayonnaise or hollandaise sauces, and other treats of French cuisine. She still cooked into her 90s but by then she was creating less epic-scale feasts and watching more TV and reading. Her big beloved cast-iron pans were becoming too heavy for her.

When Mom finally moved out of the Big House into her apartment on 91st Street and Madison Avenue, Barbara and I were only blocks away and we dropped in to visit her regularly. From time to time Mom spoke of her sister, Jean, and the days when they were girls in Baguio, eating mangos while they leaned over the porch railing behind their house so that the mango juice and slime could drip and slip into the rain forest below. Mom spoke of visiting Jean and her family in Berlin in 1928, after Jean's first baby was born. The baby was called "little Woody" though he eventually grew to be nearly 6ft 6in tall.

Mom's younger sister, Jean, married first and died first. Mom's memories of visiting her in Berlin were happy—Berlin was a vibrant European capital with avenues lined with rows of linden trees, and she savored the good times spent there with Jean and her new baby.

Jean returned to the United States to be matron of honor at Mom and Pop's wedding in Baltimore in November 1930. Within two years, Jean had moved back to the US for good when her husband—Uncle Woody to me—started work at the Federal Reserve Bank of New York. Jean had a new baby boy, Darrah. Mom was overjoyed. Jean and her two babies were living in Montclair, New Jersey, and Uncle Woody commuted to the Federal Reserve Building in the Wall Street financial district.

In 1933, Mom had staff in the house in Locust Valley where she and Pop lived while Grandmother Brewster was still in the Big House a few miles away. Mom took a break from her routine in Locust Valley and went to visit Jean in Montclair. Mom and Jean got carried away with the fun of being together as sisters again. They talked about the donkey and cart Gramps bought for them in Cuba; eating mangoes on the porch in Baguio; and the good times in Berlin just a few years before. They were giddy with being together and had a pillow fight. At one point, Jean smacked Mom with a pillow, lost her balance and fell off the bed, scratching her face on something as she fell. It was just a small scratch and they thought nothing of it. It had been a wonderful day. Mom went back to Locust Valley.

Within days, Jean was dead from a bacterial infection that would have been easily cured with penicillin, but penicillin would not be available for another decade. Mom must have felt some guilt and responsibility for her sister's death.

Mom talked with Barbara and me about the parallel between

her losing her sister and Pop losing his brother seven years earlier. "Nobody knew how to talk about something like that then. Maybe if your Pop had talked with a therapist after his brother died, it would have made a difference."

I think Mom was also speaking about herself. Maybe if she had talked with a therapist after Jean's death, it would have been easier for her to deal with the unavoidable feelings of loss and guilt. Talking with therapists was not something many people did at that time. Pop dealt with loss and painful emotions with gin and Lucky Strikes. Mom dealt with them in stoical retreat. She distanced herself from the pain, stuffed it away out of sight.

At some point in the '90s, Mom, Barbara, and I connected with another Wood cousin, Willie, in Washington. He invited the three of us to visit. While we were in DC we visited the family plot in Arlington National Cemetery, where Gramps and Omy, and other family members were buried. Among the graves was a headstone for Jean, 1903–1933. Seeing it, Mom burst into tears and, as if speaking to her dead sister, said, "Jean, I thought we would grow old together."

Mom could roll up her sleeves and run Brewster Automobiles, flex her muscles like Rosie the Riveter, and keep the family and the family business going like the children's-book character Winnie Winkle. Whatever the challenge, Mom took command like the General's daughter she was. Some of the challenges gave her migraines, but she handled them all with stoicism. At 89 she could fly through a storm over the Balkans with grace and calm in a suit, hat, and gloves, using smelling salts, as needed, to keep her heart going so she could enjoy the trip. As Dr. Marks observed, she was at times a distant goddess, who came down from Olympian heights to visit with us mortals, and as the good doctor also noted, she was still very beautiful and unwrinkled in her 90s.

Just occasionally Mom's emotions broke through—when I broke the Lalique birds, when Rosie died, when Mom stood at her sister's grave a half century after Jean's death. But, throughout life's turmoils, Mom stayed loyal to the Mets, Bill Clinton, and her children, and she soared overhead like the Audubon birds of prey she loved, observing the world and its pain from a distance, safe in the towering heights where the eagle, hawk, and falcon circle and glide.

CHAPTER 15.

Isabel the Third
(1932–2002)

Many English Women make their husbands
beggars
By high living, idlenesse, wastfullnesse, furbelowed Scarves, & scolding them from Home.

William Stoughton
Flyleaf note

My sister, Isabel, was named after our grandmother, Isabel
Erskine Brewster. Grandmother Brewster had been born in Dav-
enport, Iowa—but was intensely proud of her New England roots
in Wiscasset, Maine—and was named after her mother, also an
Isabel. Thus, my sister, who had known Grandmother Brewster,
was Isabel the Third.

Not only was Grandmother Brewster proud of her New England roots, she was also proud to bear the middle name Erskine.
It was, she told my sister, very aristocratic. Our Erskine ancestors,
she explained, were direct descendants of Scotland's Lord Erskine. There was a grain of truth in this. The Erskines were, indeed,
a Scottish clan, headed by Lord Erskine. However, the Erskines
who moved to New England in pre-Revolutionary times were
poor, illiterate members of the clan. They signed their name with
an "X" in the Wiscasset town records. But Grandmother Brewster's myth rubbed off on my sister and it became the basis of one of

her many contradictions—at once a liberal thinker she was also a proud believer in Grandmother Brewster's grandiose family story that told of lordly family roots.

Isabel was 10 years older than me. When I was eight, she was a freshman in college and I worshipped her. She was beautiful and, I believed, could do anything. When we started to ski in Vermont, she could *wedel* perfectly down the slope in tight parallel turns, while I was struggling with a snowplow and awkward, lurching, stem turns. She could sing like an opera singer, doing *coloratura* trills in soprano arias. She learned to speak Italian, and while at Smith College, spent her junior year in Florence. She could sing Verdi, Mozart, and Puccini in Italian. When she came back from Italy, she brought me a small Florentine leather cufflink box with gold embossed lines in the lid. When she gave it to me, I had no cufflinks, but I treasured it. When Isabel was home, she liked to find out everything that her baby brother had been doing, including my deepest secrets. She did not boss me around like my older brothers, but wanted to know about me, and she always listened. I confided in her. Later she confided in me.

None of Isabel's awesome attributes and accomplishments reduced Sam's and my desire to harass her. We were obnoxious little brothers to the best of our ability. When her boyfriends telephoned her at the Big House and we picked up the phone, we gave them a hard time. One year, when she came back from boarding school, we developed a plan, so that we could hear her high soprano scream rattle the windows. Our bedroom in the Big House was next to Isabel's at the end of the hall. Her bedroom had a bathroom with a tub and shower curtain, which she pulled back to step into the shower. Our bathroom had a tub with a drain. In the drain we discovered a mass of rotting hair and unidentifiable filth. Combined with similar disgusting dregs from other drains, we collected a witch's stew worthy of poor Peacham's evil spirits. We knew when Isabel planned to take a shower, and placed our revolting mess on the bottom of her tub, just behind the closed shower curtain where she was likely to step. We retreated to our bedroom and waited. As anticipated, Isabel went to her room and got ready to take a shower before being picked up by one of her many boyfriends. There was silence followed by a profoundly satisfying high-pitched scream. Whether by lying and denial or some other good fortune, we got away with it.

Isabel graduated from Miss Hall's School and then Smith College and worked as a secretary at the Rockefeller Institute in New York in the mid 1950s until she married Vance in 1956. She introduced me to Italian opera and Gilbert & Sullivan operettas, which she sang with the Blue Hill Troupe, a serious amateur Gilbert & Sullivan group in New York.

When I became interested in girls, Isabel wanted to know if I was a "tit man or a leg man." She insisted that all men are one or the other. I begged off, responding that I liked the whole package. She was not satisfied.

Like Mom, Isabel was a voracious reader, fascinated by history. With me she shared important historical information and theories: the Empress Josephine, she enlightened me, liked to have sex with Napoleon after military campaigns before he took a bath. Isabel explained that the Empress's appetite for dirty sex reflected *nostalgie pour la boue*, nostalgia for mud, meaning the primordial muck from which evolution began. *Nostalgie pour la boue* was a cultural theme, which Isabel traced from Roman historians, through French and German psychologists to Bob Dylan lyrics. My sister was outrageous fun, whether or not I understood all of her theories.

In October 1959, early in my "fifth form" or junior year at St. Paul's, one of the masters told me that I had to go to a room on the second floor of the main school building for an important call at 1:00 p.m. I do not remember whether I was given a number to call or just picked up the phone when it rang. In either case, Isabel was on the line, calling from Georgetown, where she and Vance lived while he was working in Washington for the World Bank. I had just become an uncle. Isabel was excited to tell her little brother and I was excited to hear the news. Rose Van Dine, "Rosie," was born on October 8, 1959. Although Isabel and Vance wanted more children, Rosie's birth was preceded and followed by multiple miscarriages. Rosie was to be their only child and was the center of their lives.

Back in Manhattan after the World Bank, Isabel and Vance lived on Central Park West and then Park Avenue. Rosie went to Manhattan private schools—Spence and then Nightingale—and ultimately to college at Georgetown. She was irresistible from the time she was a little girl—lively, pretty, intelligent, and adventurous.

Rosie became all the more central to Isabel's life as her marriage to Vance deteriorated. Vance had first seen Isabel when she was singing in a Gilbert & Sullivan operetta in Manhattan. His best friend from Yale, Danny, knew Isabel and introduced them. It seemed to be love at first sight—like Gramps seeing Omy stepping off the train in Buffalo. I don't know what went wrong between them, but over the years their relationship became strained.

Vance became a partner at Morgan Stanley and made more and more money. He traveled frequently for business. He joined Seawanhaka Yacht Club on Centre Island in Oyster Bay. His sailboats got bigger and bigger, culminating in a 40-foot floating living room with sails, which he named *Bel Canto*, after his and Isabel's shared love of opera. Their lives were bound together by

Rosie, but became more and more separate. When Vance was not away on business, he was often off on long summer cruises with sailing friends—Isabel did not join them. Vance had started his sailing hobby with a small day-sailing sloop, which he kept at the beach at the bottom of Smuggler's Lane near the Big House. His choice of name for his first sailboat gives some insight into his psyche—she was called *Pussy Galore.*

I married my first wife, Michelle, in Belgium in 1964, eight years after Isabel and Vance's wedding. During the week that culminated in our wedding, Michelle's cousin, Pierre, had a lunch party for us at his very grand house in the countryside outside of Brussels. There was a large crowd at the party and it was easy for anyone to drift off and tour the grounds. Vance evidently did a tour in the bushes with an attractive Belgian blonde. At one point I saw them emerge from behind a thick hedge at the edge of the lawn. Both were disheveled and rearranging their clothes.

Twelve years after Vance and Isabel were married, Michelle and I moved to Brooklyn, and Isabel came to confide in me. She had found letters written to Vance by a woman in California where Vance spent a significant amount of time ostensibly on business for Morgan Stanley. Isabel asked me to keep the letters for her. One included photographs of a boy.

"See how much he looks like you," the letter said.

The boy, perhaps seven or eight years old in the pictures, wore a blue Civil War uniform and was the spitting image of Vance. At the time Isabel gave me the letters, she also disclosed that Vance had been withdrawing money from a trust they had created and funded for Rosie.

Whatever tensions and affairs undermined Isabel and Vance's relationship, they both loved Rosie, who grew and flourished and graduated from Georgetown in 1981. After graduating, she hitchhiked through South America, some of the time alone. On her return to the US, she began graduate school in journalism at Washington University in St. Louis. In 1982, during a summer break from graduate school, she visited Michelle and me and our children for a short stay at our farm in Pennsylvania. It was the last time I saw her.

After Rosie flew the nest, Isabel and Vance's life together continued on Park Avenue and in the greenhouse, which they had converted into a weekend and summer home on the family property in Glen Cove. The potting shed, a small building attached to the north end of the long glass greenhouse, became the kitchen. Initially, the greenhouse itself was both bedroom and living room, until Isabel and Vance added a one-story annex next to the kitchen, in order to create a master bedroom, and eventually a second story with Rosie's bedroom and a guest room. The long greenhouse itself had curved glass eaves, and heating pipes along the walls beneath tables for growing orchids. Near the peak of the greenhouse the glass was louvered and could be opened and closed by cranking wheels positioned at the bottom of long rods that extended down to within human reach. Above the heating pipes, Isabel and Vance built cabinets and shelves, which he covered with ceramic owls that he collected, and eclectic bric-a-brac that he and Isabel found on their trips together. A straw monkey from a trip to Africa with Rosie hung by his right hand from one of the window crank wheels. Vance laid black and white tile on the long floor and did much of the carpentry himself. He tinted the slanted glass panels in the greenhouse roof to reduce the glare and summer heat. They added air-conditioning. Off the south end of the greenhouse, a large willow tree planted after Rosie was born provided a shady outdoor seating area.

The greenhouse was a masterpiece, a great place for dinner on a hot summer night. Eventually, Isabel and Vance added a swimming pool along the hedge on the far side of the lawn where our World War II vegetable garden had been, and a tennis court where the orchard had been between the Big House and the cottages along Crescent Beach Road. The grape arbor remained in place on the north side of Isabel and Vance's lawn. The path on the south side also remained. This was the path by which Isabel walked to the Big House to visit with Mom, and which Mom used to walk to the greenhouse to see Isabel or clip peonies to bring back to the Big House. As in my childhood, the path was still flanked by rows of peonies, next to the raspberry and asparagus patch.

Vance continued to go on his month-long summer cruises in *Bel Canto*, usually joining a flotilla with friends in their own boats, and sometimes making it as far as Northeast Harbor, Maine. Michelle and I spent most of our weekends and vacations at our farm, down the road from Sam, in Pennsylvania, but we saw Isabel and Vance occasionally at the greenhouse in the summer and more often in Manhattan in the winter, where they were regular opera goers. There was palpable tension between them. Isabel developed a painful case of Crohn's disease, which worsened over time. She still could be outrageous and fun to talk with, but not as often. Her mood darkened. She spent more time in her bedroom, both in Glen Cove and Manhattan. Visits with her increasingly involved sitting in a chair next to her bed.

My separating from Michelle in 1983 and moving in with Mary enraged Isabel. Her anger upset me. I do not know if she felt threatened by my leaving Michelle or if she believed her little brother had made a bad decision. She never mentioned any possibility of leaving Vance, regardless of the painful confidences that she shared with me. She may have been afraid of being left alone in the empty nest that Rosie had flown years before. I do not know why, but Isabel was clearly angry with me.

Our relationship was under this strain, when she called me at my desk at Moses & Singer on August 23, 1983. Rosie's plane had crashed. No more information was available. While in graduate school in St. Louis, Rosie's love of adventure and risky thrills had continued. She became a pilot and then developed a passion for stunt flying. Vance had bought her the stunt-flying plane in which she crashed with her instructor. Isabel and Vance were at the greenhouse trying to obtain information. The plane had crashed but had Rosie survived? I said I would take the next train to Glen Cove. It was a Wednesday and I had to hand off legal work, including a court appearance. I spoke briefly with a colleague at Moses & Singer who agreed to cover for me and I headed for the Long Island Railroad. I was on the Long Island side of Penn Station within a half hour. An hour and three quarters on the train and I was in Glen Cove. It was not fast enough. By the time I arrived Isabel was in a rage. Why had it taken me so long? Waiting for me and, far more importantly, waiting for information about Rosie must have seemed like an eternity in hell.

Neither Rosie nor her instructor survived. They were both killed instantly when the plane crashed. The investigation concluded that the new plane had had a mechanical failure. The plane crashed in a wheat field in Boonville, Missouri, about 150 miles from St. Louis. I was in the greenhouse when the call came through. Isabel or Vance asked me to tell Mom. I walked up the path to the Big House and up the stairs to Mom's room to tell her the devastating news. She burst into tears. Mom grieved most of all for her living daughter, crying "Poor Isabel, poor Isabel."

Isabel lived another 20 years, dying in November 2002. She outlived Mom by just over a year, but the Isabel I had known died with Rosie. Her Crohn's disease became progressively worse. She eventually had a colostomy and lived on with an ostomy bag. Complications from the Crohn's disease, lung cancer from a habit of chain-smoking cigarillos, and severe depression had ravaged her. Without Rosie, she said, "I have nothing to live for."

For years after Rosie's death, Isabel appeared angry about my divorce from Michelle. Barbara and I met two years after my 1987 divorce and married in 1990, but Isabel wanted the clock turned back to 1982, before Michelle and I separated and when Rosie was still alive. Both she and Vance refused to come to our wedding. Barbara eventually won them over with kindness and perseverance.

In her last years, Isabel was in and out of the hospital. One crisis led to her being placed in an induced coma that lasted for weeks at Mount Sinai Hospital. On other occasions when she was in the hospital, Isabel was sometimes psychotic from medication. Once we took our daughter, Darrah, to Mount Sinai Hospital to cheer Isabel up. Darrah was five. She was scared and fidgeted in a chair next to the bed. Isabel yelled at her. We never took Darrah again.

Vance kept working and sailing *Bel Canto*. In spite of everything, I liked Vance. He had been part of the family for 50 years and we had too small a family to lose anyone. He was easy to be with, but hard to know. Whatever lay beneath the surface, he never revealed it. After Rosie's death, he showed less visible damage than Isabel, but there must have been great hidden damage and unspoken pain. Rosie was the apple of his eye and it was he who had bought her the plane that killed her. After Isabel died he lived on for another eight years, dying in a retirement home in San Diego, near his sister and her children. I visited him there, as did his California nieces and nephew. It is possible that the California son whose picture was in the letters entrusted to me by Isabel also visited him.

After Rosie's death, while Vance and Isabel were both alive, they seemed to compete with each other, spending money as self-medication. After Isabel died, Barbara helped Vance to clear out her closets. New designer clothes hung in her walk-in master bedroom closet, the closets in Rosie's bedroom, the guest room, and the front hall. Tags were still attached to the collars and sleeves—evidently Isabel had never worn any of them.

But, in spite of her extravagant spending, Isabel was not one of the women on the flyleaf of the witchcraft judge's book, who made "their husbands beggars by high living." She was no more extravagant than Vance. She did not "scold" him "from Home," regardless of his unending infidelities. Isabel and Vance chose to stay with each other spending money they no longer had. As Vance's closest friend said, they burned through money "like drunken sailors on shore leave." They out-spent their retirement income and Vance borrowed from friends. Unpaid bills lay in ever growing piles in their apartment.

When Isabel died, she was a far cry from the pretty girl who skied the Vermont slopes in tight parallel turns, spoke Italian, and sang arias with *coloratura* flourishes. By turns an outrageous snob and a wild liberal, she was never dull. But Rosie's death came to a life already in emotional and physical pain. For even the strongest and most positive parent, a child's death is the hardest blow. How does a parent survive? A character in a Robert Frost poem says, "The best way out is always through." Isabel just could not make it through. She disintegrated, very slowly, before our eyes.

Isabel, Vance, and Rosie, all three now reduced to ashes, are together in the garden of St. John's of Lattingtown, the church where Isabel and Vance were married. It is just a few minutes from the Big House by bicycle or in the old Brewster automobile with patent-leather fenders. I see Pop crank up the 1919 Brewster to drive Isabel to her wedding. Sam and I were in the church waiting when Pop and Isabel got there, but as if I stood outside watching, the sight of them driving up the lane to St. John's comes back to me now like a thin slice of the moon, glimpsed or only imagined, between moving clouds.

CHAPTER 16.

Sam Vanishes over the Horizon Again
(1971–2017)

As soon as he was born, he cried not as other
babes use to do, Miez, miez, miez, miez, but
with a high, sturdy, and big voice shouted
about, "SOME DRINK, SOME DRINK,
SOME DRINK", as inviting all the world to
drink with him.

On the birth of the giant Gargantua
François Rabelais, 1534

SAM WAS my older brother by about two years. He was also taller,
bigger, smarter, and louder than me. He was bossy, sometimes a
bully. He once told his best friend, Willy, that I was "the worst little brother in the world." That hurt. It was before I went to Green
Vale School in Glen Head and made friends, before I had a bicycle
that could take me away from the Big House to exotic places like
Bayville and Oyster Bay. Before all of it, Sam was my best friend,
my only friend. But the combination of his physical and mental
prowess meant that battles of brain or brawn between us rarely
went well for me.

In spite of our fights, I loved Sam. We were close and did
almost everything together when we were little—archery, jousting
with garden stakes and garbage-pail lids found beneath the back
porch, swimming ever longer distances in the Sound, exploring the
swamp behind the beach, and bringing home captured frogs and

mice. Sometimes there was a blurry line between Sam the mean bully and Sam my best friend. We both spent time doing cannon balls and diving into the Sound off the dock at the beach. Once he dared me to dive through a large jellyfish, but I had learned a thing or two by then and did not do it.

Sam and I were very close until 1954, when he went away to boarding school at St. Paul's in Concord, New Hampshire. Then he disappeared over the horizon. Sam was to disappear over my horizon a number of times. I sometimes wondered if he was trying to get away from me—perhaps he really meant it when he said I was "the worst little brother in the world."

When Gramps died in 1955 and I felt very alone in the Big House, Sam was away at school. When I got to St. Paul's two years later, Sam had gone to England to attend boarding school at Harrow. Later, after dropping out of Columbia and working in a gypsum plant in the Bronx, Sam disappeared in Germany for a period of time. But each time he disappeared over the horizon, he eventually came back. With his disappearances and reappearances, our relationship ebbed and flowed like the tides at the beach at the bottom of Smuggler's Lane.

In 1971, Sam came back into my life. Sometime after I returned from Beirut following Tom's acquittal in Turkey, I got a call from Sam, saying that there was a great farm for sale five minutes down the road from his place in Cold Springs, Pennsylvania.

The land was a gem. New on the market, it was on top of a hill bordering thousands of acres of "Pennsylvania Game Lands" managed for wildlife, hunting, and fishing. The state land ran the length of the south and west sides of the property and was easily accessible from the property, but not from any nearby public road. It sloped down a hillside through woods to a remote trout stream—the west branch of the Dyberry Creek—where you could fish in solitude and catch brook trout all day long.

The farm itself was a mix of fields, pasture, and woodland nearly surrounding Carr Pond, a deep 30-acre pond gouged out of the earth by glaciers tens of thousands of years ago. Neighbors claimed to have measured anywhere from 30 to 50 feet of depth in the center of Carr Pond. A marsh and peat bog lay at the south end of the pond, where we later found a 400-year-old Native American dugout canoe perfectly preserved and hidden in the peat. The Leni Lenape used the canoe to trap beaver to sell to the English and Dutch settlers. The English and Dutch had exhausted the beaver supply closer to the coast by about 1650 and began to trade with tribes as far inland as the upper Delaware. The University of Pennsylvania carbon-dated the dugout canoe to that time. It had been hollowed out by both stone and iron tools, showing that its mid-17th-century builder had used European tools, as well as the traditional stone tools and fire. About 150 years later, the land and pond frontage was deeded, in lieu of pay, to an American soldier named Carr at the end of the Revolution—there had been more land than money to pay soldiers.

I went to see the farm the weekend after Sam called. The 19th-century farmhouse—purchased from a Sears Roebuck Catalogue before 1900—had a sagging roof and was about to cave into its foundation, but the land was beautiful and less than a three-hour drive from where my growing family and I lived in Brooklyn.

I liked the idea of being close to my older brother. He was no longer the chubby 10- or 11-year-old with whom I found the witchcraft judge's books. He was now 6ft 2in tall and weighed 300 pounds, give or take a few. He was larger than life, had always been larger than life. Although I was studious and always at the top of my class in school, Sam was a near-genius from the time he was a baby, pulling himself up on the bars of his playpen and using uncanny infant mechanical skills to dismantle the playpen and then crawl away.

In all things relating to science, math, and engineering—from his playpen dismantling onward—Sam was light-years ahead of me. I think he was probably the smartest human being I ever met. He was curious and analytical—a polymath who knew something about everything. I envied his brilliance. I was no polymath. I told myself that at least I went deeper into the comparatively few things I knew anything about. I could never compete with him in anything relating to science or math or any of the wide range of subjects he knew about, but I plodded along and stayed the educational course through college and law school.

As much as Sam loved learning, he rebelled at formal education. When he graduated from St. Paul's, he "forgot" to mail in his college application to Princeton. This upset Pop, which I think was Sam's plan, conscious or not. Sam did get into Columbia where he went but said it was boring. He dropped out after his freshman year.

It was around that time that Sam and I started talking seriously about buying a farm. We both wanted to get away from the Big House in Glen Cove, to put distance between us and the social scene of Long Island's Gold Coast. We also needed to escape the memories of Pop's shakes and depression.

When Sam bought his farm, Pop was still alive. When I bought mine he was no longer with us, but still I yearned for distance, to escape the memories of his final months in the Big House. For months in 1969 Pop lay dying in a hospital bed in the sitting room next to the master bedroom, where Mom still slept. They had shared that room and its large mahogany sleigh bed for almost 40 years. Pop's slow death had come with an unforgettable smell.

I wanted rural air to carry it downwind, along with the scent of the gin martinis and the big ashtray filled with Lucky Strike butts.

Sam and I were not consistent in our desire to distance ourselves from the Big House and its advantages, either before or after Pop's death. A desire for separation in principle did not stop us in practice from taking over the property to throw a wild weekend house party while Mom and Pop were in Europe—we could play while the parental cats were away, but we still longed to get far away from the Evil Spirits.

I don't think either of us would have recognized it but our attraction to rural life probably had something to do with Pop. Pop wore baggy pants and did not look all that different from the dairy-farming cousins we met in Vermont. He loved driving his Jeep station wagon and Ford pick-up truck around the Vermont dirt roads. Inspired by the livestock on our lawn during the war and then by a book called *Four Acre Farm*, Pop decided to have a chicken coop built for 100 Rhode Island Reds below our orchard. His main reason behind the scheme was so that we boys could learn, hands-on, where food came from by feeding the hens and collecting their eggs every day. In addition to the Rhode Island Reds, Pop bought a handful of Speckled Bantams, just because they were fun and beautiful.

For Sam, the chicken coop in Glen Cove and the surplus eggs that Mom sold to Bedrick's Market on nearby Landing Road foreshadowed the chicken business he launched on his farm in Cold Springs, but he did not stop at a chicken coop for 100 chickens. On his Pennsylvania farm he had a coop that looked as long as a football field. It was home to 10,000 white Leghorns that he bought as chicks. Under contract with a factory-laying operation Sam raised the chicks until they were ready to lay. Then they were shipped off to the factory farm.

Never as edible as Pop's Rhode Island Reds, when they left Sam's farm, his prolific Leghorns could each produce nearly 300 large white eggs a year. Sam put up a second giant coop for another 10,000 chicks—a total of 20,000 birds. It was typical Sam. He did nothing in a small way. As teenagers, when we were watching TV late on a Saturday night, he would go into the kitchen for a snack. One night he ate half a roast beef that Mom had planned to serve for Sunday lunch. Sam's appetite for food and life alike was gargantuan.

By the time Sam and I started talking about buying farmland in the mid 1960s he had decided on full-time rural living. I, on the other hand, was looking for a part-time rural escape while I practiced law in New York. We did some research. We got a pair of compasses and put the sharp end into Manhattan on a map that covered New York, Connecticut, Massachusetts, New Jersey, and Pennsylvania. Then we drew 50-, 100- and 150-mile circles around the city. Our research showed that the price of farmland was affordable for us if we were willing to drive two hours from the city. We started looking at ads in the United Farms Agency catalogs for land within our affordable circles. I spotted an ad for a nearly 200-acre farm in Cold Springs, Pennsylvania, complete with a house with double chimneys that had been a cattle "drovers" inn in the early 1800s. Sam was ready to make the move and bought it.

Now, five years later, I had decided that it would be good to be a mile down a dirt road from my brother. The only catch was that Michelle and I had bought and renovated a brownstone in Brooklyn and already owned a farm in New York State seven hours away from the city. We had no money to buy land in Pennsylvania. I would have to borrow to bridge the gap between the purchase of the new farm and the sale of my land in western New York. If not, someone else might snap up the farm before I could put the money together.

Borrowing went against the advice Pop had given me in his toast at my wedding in Brussels. He had dusted off his French and laboriously translated Polonius's speech to his son, Laertes, in *Hamlet*. At the wedding, holding his glass of champagne, Pop urged me: "Neither a borrower nor a lender be." In spite of the gin and Lucky Strikes, Pop did his best to teach me the same lessons that Henry Peacham had once laid out in *The Worth Of A Penny*. I did not listen. By 1971, Pop had been gone for two years. I borrowed the money from Mom, who was characteristically supportive and generous. Plus she liked the idea of my being just down the road from Sam. And so I bought the farm on Carr Pond. With another $150 I bought a working World War II Jeep, which the seller had stored in his barn. The farm in western New York sold quickly and I repaid Mom.

For the next decade on Carr Pond, I was closer to Sam in every way than at any time since we had fired spitballs around the living room with miniature brass cannons. We never had an idyllic *Brady Bunch* or *Leave It to Beaver* relationship. Sam and I were brothers separated by just a couple of years. We were competitive. "My cannon shoots a spitball farther than your cannon!" (I don't remember for sure, but Sam, being a better engineer, probably made a cannon that shot spitballs farther than mine.)

My own pushback against conventional life in New York was less spectacular than Sam's had been. I did not enjoy being a Wall Street lawyer. Working in ship and aircraft financing, in particular, was, as one of my friends at Milbank Tweed said, "like sailing too long into the sun." In 1974, I left Wall Street and moved on to a job that I loved at the US Attorney's Office in Brooklyn. Within weeks after drafting my last ship mortgage at Milbank, I was trying a narcotics case in front of a jury in federal court. Over the next decade, when I wasn't preparing for trial or trying a case, Michelle loaded up the station wagon at the end of the day on Friday and we headed to Carr Pond for the weekend with Sylvia and Scott and our German shorthaired pointer, Chloe.

In Cold Springs I saw a lot of Sam, his wife Peg, and Robin and Bobby, Peg's children from her previous marriage. In addition to the 20,000 chickens, Sam and Peg had family farm animals—a flock of sheep, some pigs, a donkey, a horse, a ferret with terrible body odor, a German shepherd named Buddy—who hunted woodchucks—and a snow-white goat named Tulip. Tulip was irresistible and very friendly.

Just as Chloe liked to be with me, so Tulip the goat liked to be with Sam. Chloe liked to ride around with me in my 1944 Jeep. Sam was similarly accompanied by Tulip. He removed the front passenger seat from his old Saab, so that Tulip could ride with him wherever he went, including to Honesdale, the county seat and nearest place for shopping, a half hour down the road. Having a top speed of about 30 miles an hour, my World War II Jeep took forever to get to Honesdale, but Chloe and I could go anywhere on the logging roads around Cold Springs. And, unlike Tulip, Chloe could find game birds. Sam's German shepherd, Buddy, liked to hunt and kill woodchucks, but he was no better at finding grouse and woodcock than Tulip.

Sam and I took Chloe and our double-barreled shotguns and went grouse hunting in the mountain laurels on the edge of the swamp at the back end of his property. We got off some shots, but never hit any birds. When we jumped them, the grouse threw us off-balance with their thundering takeoffs and then disappeared behind the thick-growth laurels or a stone wall or some evergreens—we would have gotten just as many grouse had we taken Buddy or Tulip.

Sam and I engaged in other hunter-gatherer activities. We collected wild leeks ("ramps") in the woods and wild potatoes ("wapatoo") in the marshy edges of Carr Pond. Unlike an Idaho or Long Island potato a wapatoo is the size of a pea and harvesting enough for a meal expends as many calories as you gain from eating them. We also hunted for mushrooms. I had been a student of mushrooms (mycologist) and a mushroom eater (mycophagist) for 10 years without killing myself or anyone else. I had a small library of books about mushrooms. I got Sam hooked. He went into mushroom hunting in a big way. And, of course, we were competitive about it. We did not tell each other where to find all of our best mushroom spots in the woods and fields around our farms.

My neighbor, dairy farmer John Pykus, taught me about a wonderful mushroom called a "stumpy" that his family found and used to make mushroom sauce in Poland. The family re-discovered stumpies in Pennsylvania, after emigrating to the United States and moving to the Pennsylvania hills, where they became farmers near Polish relatives and friends who worked in the coal mines around Scranton and Carbondale. I told Sam about stumpies and we found huge quantities of them. We looked them up and then cooked them up—*armillaria mellea* or honey mushrooms. Stumpies, or honey mushrooms, are high on the list of good mushrooms, just below the golden chanterelles I found in the woods on the other side of Carr Pond or the morels I used to find along Smuggler's Lane in Glen Cove.

Sam and I were interested in making cider to go with the mushrooms and, indeed, everything else. I made some in a 15-gallon oak barrel with a valve in the bunghole. I had bought the set-up in a winemaking store in Little Italy. Once again, it became a competition. My barrel and valve afforded me a somewhat controlled fermentation resulting in golden, clear cider. Sam's cider was a little cloudy. He made it in 5-gallon jars, which stood fermenting in the corners of the rooms of his house.

Sam also made elderberry and dandelion wine, which sat around his house in jars. The elderberry wine was too sweet for me and the dandelion wine was sickening—imagine horse piss. I loved Sam but the single most nauseating meal I have ever eaten was at his house in Cold Springs: sautéed hog kidneys with a ketchup-based sauce, washed down with a choice of elderberry or dandelion wine.

Those years on our neighboring farms followed a seasonal rhythm. In the summer I fly-fished for trout in the Dyberry Creek. In the fall Chloe and I hunted grouse and woodcock. Michelle and I and the kids sometimes came to the farm in the winter to cross-country ski on the endless miles of logging roads, enjoying the heavy snowfall that predictably came to the northeastern corner of Pennsylvania every year. In the winter, when we stayed in Brooklyn, I tied flies with fur and feathers harvested from fall hunting, and sometimes supplemented with a scrap of muskrat fur or a bucktail given to me by a neighbor.

I generally supplied my own bucktail, since almost every year I bagged a deer with a bow and arrow from a tree stand in my woods or the old orchard at the bottom of the field below our house. The best thing about bow hunting was what you observed as you sat still in a tree stand—more than once I saw a fox training her kits to hunt and once a ruffed grouse sat next to me on the limb where I perched, unaware that I was not part of the tree. Venison roasts, chops, steaks, burgers, and scrapple became staples for my family, adding to the dozen or so woodcock, grouse, and occasional pheasant Chloe and I brought home. No part of a deer went to waste. The horns became knife handles and buttons. The hides became suede.

The rural pattern and my close relationship with Sam continued into the late 1980s. But things started to change after he and Peg divorced. Sam met and married Eliza Lahm, who lived nearby on the Delaware River in Callicoon. I liked Eliza. She and Sam seemed happy together and I was happy for Sam.

Financially, Eliza was a godsend for Sam. The chicken business was not easy, thanks to fluctuations in the price of eggs and chicken mortality, and like the young heirs in *The Worth Of A Penny*, Sam had galloped through family money. Eliza was the cavalry that came to the rescue. Her father's family owned the Lamston Department Store chain. Her mother, Dorothy Fields, was a famous songwriter who collaborated with Jerome Kern and Irving Berlin. She wrote the lyrics for *Annie Get Your Gun*, other Broadway shows, and more than 400 songs including "I Can't Give You Anything but Love Baby" and "I'm in the Mood for Love." Royalties flowed like a great river into Eliza's bank account.

As a newly single man after Michelle and I separated in 1983, I spent time with Sam and Eliza. Eliza was charming and fun but some time after Barbara entered my life in 1989, Eliza started to have unexpected outbursts. She became more and more possessive of Sam. She seemed to want to drive away the people who were closest to him. Her outbursts became more and more frequent and ever more unpredictable. A few drinks made things worse. A simple request for her to "Pass the butter, please," or almost anything could trigger an explosion.

Whatever the causes of Eliza's outbursts, my relationship with Sam did not survive October 6, 1990, the day that Barbara and I were married. In the days leading up to the ceremony, Eliza's erratic behavior continued, and Sam and I said unforgivable things to each other. Sam and Eliza refused to come to the wedding, and I felt that I never wanted to speak to Sam again. Mom and Barbara's family came to our wedding, but Isabel, Tom, and Sam were not there. Tom was in Nicosia, Cyprus. Isabel was in a deepening depression, years after Rosie's death. Plus she had felt threatened by my divorce and sided with Michelle. With Sam it was different. For reasons Barbara and I never understood, Eliza drove a wedge between Sam and me—I was hurt, sad, and in a rage.

Three years went by before I had any contact with him. By 1993, Isabel and Vance had become more and more stressed financially and had decided to sell the Big House, which they had bought from Mom in the hope of keeping it in the family forever. The anticipated sale motivated Mom to make some decisions about the huge inventory of personal possessions that filled it. She was then 93 years old and had watched with sadness and disappointment as cracks in her children's relationships grew. She decided to do what she could to mitigate any conflict over the family possessions after she died. She orchestrated a family meeting in which each of us would take turns, in rotating order of seniority, and put our names on the particular items we wanted.

She asked for help to organize the family meeting. I had just taken a year off from litigation practice in a spectacularly unsuccessful attempt to write the great American novel and had some time on my hands. I said I would help her.

In my abortive effort as a novelist, I had become computer savvy, a fast touch-typist on my Mac and familiar with other applications for the computer. I created a database, listing and numbering every item in every room in the Big House. As to each item, I could later enter whether Isabel, Tom, Sam, or I had chosen it. I could sort the database in various ways before and after the family meeting.

After the meeting, the computer could spit out lists of what each of us had chosen. I created the database, listing 957 items in the 35 rooms. I photographed each item, creating an album of pictures keyed to the numbered items in the database. Mom, Isabel, Tom, Sam, and I each had a copy of the database listing and a duplicate album of the photographs.

Some items were already covered by gift letters written by Pop long before he died. He had given each of us a particular family heirloom that he wanted us to have—almost entirely from the house in Wiscasset, Maine. For example, in his letter to me he said that he wanted me to have a tall-case grandfather's clock, made in Boston or the North Shore of Massachusetts around 1780. Within the family it was known as "Aunt Sally's clock."

But the heirloom we all imagined to have the greatest monetary value was not Aunt Sally's clock, but a mid-18th-century mahogany blockfront desk. It had belonged to Aunt Sally's father, our many times great-grandfather, Judge Thomas Rice, who graduated from Harvard in the late 1750s with a degree in divinity, medicine, and law. Armed with his degree, he could castigate, amputate, or litigate. He chose the last option and moved to Wiscasset from Boston, where he became a Colonial judge after the British victory at Quebec in 1759.

The blockfront desk had a secret compartment for hiding money or valuable papers. It also had a notable salacious feature: there were two drawers in the center of the desk above the writing surface and in front of the secret compartment. The two drawers were adorned with the figure of a Puritan man. His upper body, waist-up, was carved on the top drawer. His lower body, waist-down, was carved on the bottom drawer. The brass knob, to pull out the bottom drawer, was between the Puritan's legs, as if he had unbuttoned his pants and pulled out his tool to relieve himself.

Sam claimed that the blockfront desk had been earmarked for him. He said he had lost Pop's letter but insisted that the desk was meant for him. Sam may have been being deceitful or his memory may have tricked him, or perhaps it was just wishful thinking. In any event Pop had kept copies of his gift letters, which we found in a shoebox in his closet. As the copies showed, Pop had, in fact, earmarked the desk for Tom.

Sam's behavior that day increased my sense of betrayal, even though it impacted Tom, not me. On his side, Sam was suspicious of the whole rotating selection process I had helped Mom to create. Sam did not trust it and came to the family meeting armed with a camcorder to document any fraudulent maneuvers and to record any evidence that Mom might have lost her marbles. There was nothing of interest for Sam's camcorder to record. Mom presided patiently over the process until we had gone through hundreds of the items in the database and reached the end of all of the conceivably valuable items. "That's enough," Mom announced. The tense family meeting ended. Sam and his camcorder went back to Pennsylvania.

I did not speak with Sam again until Mom's funeral in the winter of 2001, more than seven years later and barely spoke to him then. Again and again after our wedding in 1990, before and after the 1993 family meeting, before and after Mom's funeral in 2001, Barbara tried to patch the rift. "Don't you want to call Sam?" "He is your brother." "Why don't you call him?" She kept trying. I did not listen.

As part of our divorce settlement, Michelle had kept the brownstone in Brooklyn and I had kept the farm. I sold the house that she and I had built on the farm and built a primitive cabin with a hand-pump well and an outhouse in the woods near Carr Pond. Barbara and I stayed in the cabin from time to time. Barbara continued to work on me to make peace with Sam. Sadly, I didn't. Eventually, in 1997, I sold the cabin and the land and Barbara and I bought an apartment in the city.

The farm at Carr Pond was a special place. Before selling, I gave a conservation easement to the Nature Conservancy so that the woods, fields, and glacial pond would stay much as they were when Sam and I had hunted mushrooms, grouse, and wapatoo. Chloe, my first hunting dog, is buried among the aspen on the far side of the pond, along with a piece of my heart. Carr Pond and Sam were no longer part of my life.

Sixteen years after Mom died, long after I sold the farm, I got a call from Sam's stepdaughter Robin. Through the years she had overcome Eliza's efforts to push her away from Sam. Robin was an inspiration. I should have emulated her and listened to Barbara. Sam was important to Robin just as he was to me. Robin had fought to maintain her relationship with Sam and, to that end, struggled mightily to establish a viable relationship with Eliza. I, on the other hand, sulked in my tent like Achilles. I had no Trojans to battle, just a brother with whom I refused to make peace.

Robin's call in 2017 brought me out of my Homeric rage. She called to let me know that Sam had had a devastating stroke and was in the hospital. He wanted to speak with me. Barbara urged me to do it. It did not take much urging. Robin called back when she was at Sam's bedside and put him on the phone. I remember Sam struggling to speak. I said, "I love you, Sam" and he responded, "I love you too." I got ready to drive to the hospital the following day, but he died that night.

A few days later, Barbara and I drove to Sam's funeral in Honesdale. Before we left New York Robin and I talked about the funeral on the phone and about who would be speaking. I am not usually at a loss for words when it comes to a toast or even a eulogy but I had no words for this. I could not speak. In the end Tom spoke, as did Peg's children.

Eliza left the church in Honesdale before the service was over to go to the bar where a buffet and drinks had been laid on for everyone. She had passed me on her way into the church before the service and I passed her sitting at the bar as we left to drive home to New York. I could bring myself to say nothing more than "Sorry for your loss."

There were other familiar faces in the church and in the bar. I got an update on Sam's life over the past few years. One of Robin's children told stories about Sam driving him around the country roads in the Porsche he had bought after gas was discovered on his farm. Good for Sam. He might have thumbed his nose at Pop by forgetting to mail in his college application to Princeton, but like me, he inherited Pop's love for cars. I was glad for his good fortune but sad that I had spent no time with him in his Porsche-driving days. I still picture him in the beaten-up Saab with Tulip riding shotgun and poking her snow-white head up through the open moonroof. I am grateful for the short phone call I had with Sam the day before he died. I am grateful that the Rabelaisian giant came back over the horizon for just a few minutes before he vanished for the last time. He was a big part of my life. We found the witchcraft judge's books together. There were times when we did everything together. We competed with bows and arrows, small brass spitball cannons, mushrooms and cider, and everything else. I fought with Sam and I loved him.

CHAPTER 17.

The Circle
(now and future)

Like all generations gone before,
You and I are ashes and ghosts.
Whether the Gods in heaven
Will let tomorrow follow today,
No one but the Gods can say.

Horace, Odes, *IV, 7*

IN THE SMALL family Zoom video-call with my Cousin Lisa last April Lisa said, "You should write this stuff down." The result of Lisa's prompting makes me think of a circle, the Native American process in which a talking piece, such as an eagle feather, is passed around a circle and only the holder of the talking piece speaks. Lisa handed me the talking piece and I have held it and told these stories.

Circles loom large in my recent life. For the last several years I have worked with colleagues using a circle to teach classes in New York prisons. It may sound hokey, but there is magic in circles, even for sophisticated New Yorkers on both sides of a prison's walls. There is no hierarchy. No teacher's desk faces the class. Rules are not imposed from the outside or by anyone in the circle. As the talking piece moves from hand to hand, stories of life experience are shared. As those stories of shared humanity are told and circle round follows circle round, trust and a sense of community develop. The circle grows in strength and wisdom.

In a mystic way both the living and the dead may join the circle. The chairs in the circle may be figuratively pushed further apart, so that someone absent can join when invoked by someone present. One speaker may name an inspirational but long-dead grandparent who would add strength and wisdom. Another may name a living child, lost and struggling with life's worst issues, who might receive the circle's strength and wisdom.

Stories of life experience and shared humanity can be told in a circle or a book, but there are differences. A book usually finishes with "The End." Henry Peacham's *The Worth Of A Penny* finishes with the Latin word *FINIS*.

I cannot think of Peacham without thinking about his and Stoughton's obsession with money and my own ambivalent feelings about it. I have, to some extent, reconciled my own conflicts. I no longer see money as the evil trump card played by the Devil to win the game, but simply as a utilitarian thing. You need money to buy groceries and pay rent. This is a fact, which has been obvious to almost everyone on the planet except me. Peacham himself captures the utilitarian essence I have finally come to accept:

For a penny you may buy a fair Cucumber, but not a breast of Mutton, except if it be multiplied.

As I near eight decades of life, I finally recognize that money is necessary, not even a necessary evil, just a neutral utilitarian necessity. At long last and after much galloping through it, I finally concur with Peacham.

But I digress…

Unlike a book, a circle has no end. I like this. As a white-haired, white-skinned, Anglo-Saxon Protestant senior citizen, I am part of what is left of the smallest splinter of the richly diverse society sprouted and grown from the "Choice Grains" scattered in the wilderness by a providential God. When I and others in my small group of relics die, a representative number of us should be stuffed as an exhibit behind glass at the Natural History Museum on Central Park West in Manhattan.

The only living person I know who comes from a smaller splinter of America's diverse society is my oldest friend, Dimitri, whose family came to the United States from the White Russian diaspora of counts and countesses, princes and princesses that scattered around the world after the Russian Revolution. Perhaps Dimitri should join me in an adjoining exhibit at the Natural History Museum.

My purpose in writing this little book has been not to document, much less glorify, any splinter or fragment of society. I mean only to tell a few stories, some comical, some sad or tragic, but in every case stories of universal human experience. When stories are shared in a circle as the talking piece is passed around, regardless of the age, gender, or race of those present, a bond is created. Rather than being exclusive, the circle is inclusive. It is both intimate and infinite. When the holders of the talking piece tell stories from the heart and others listen without interruption or judgment, they become connected like the circle itself. They experience the connection with each other and with all humanity. There is no "us and them." There is only "us." The circle is the world.

Within the circle we are all linked by our fragile mortality. Horace speaks of it in the ode quoted at the beginning of this chapter. So, too, does Henry Peacham. Peacham ends his book on *The Worth Of A Penny* by bursting into celebratory French:

Since we are born, we must live, Vivions nous, *let us live as
well, as merrily as we can in these hardest times...*

His words are prophetic—everyone in America and on the
entire planet has been dealing with "these hardest times" caused
by the pandemic.

Sometimes unbearably hard times may lead to the convening of
one or more sessions or rounds of a circle. If there is a future round
I would like to invite William Stoughton to join us. I would like to
hear more about his story. As is common practice food and drink,
as well as stories, may be shared. If no one minds I would welcome
Stoughton to bring hot chocolate and perhaps he will not mind if
some of us bring wine.

I also put Judge Stoughton on notice that if we come together
in our circle, I will include all the important women in my life,
asking one or two for reconciliation and forgiveness, or at least
understanding. I know this may be hard. Of course, the inclusion
of women may be hard for Judge Stoughton, but after all, there
are now women at Harvard, that historic college which so greatly
benefited from Stoughton's riches and love. Times have changed;
perhaps the judge's views have changed as well.

But it is Saturday, the usual day for me to wind Aunt Sally's
clock. I need a few minutes to do that. When I come back, I will
pass the talking piece so others can tell their stories.

ACKNOWLEDGMENTS

I am deeply indebted to my wife, Barbara, and to my wonderful colleague, Professor Lela P. Love of the Benjamin Cardozo School of Law. Both Barbara and Lela read and provided valuable comments on each chapter of *Witchcraft Legacy*, as I turned them out during the COVID-19 lockdown. When the lockdown started, Lela and I were in the middle of using the circle process to teach a conflict resolution and negotiation class for prisoners in Queensboro Correctional Facility, a New York State prison in New York City. The pandemic interrupted us and the energetic and talented law students on our teaching team. All visitors were suddenly locked out of the prisons and we had to cut short our work. But the COVID lockdown doors that slammed shut opened other doors and gave me the time to have Zoom cocktails with my cousin Lisa Tracy, who told me to write this stuff down. Thank you, Lisa, for the nudge.

I am thankful to the small group who, in addition to Barbara and Lela and Lisa, generously read and commented on my drafts: Abigail Katowitz, Liz Appel, Daniel Montana, James Rasenberger, Charlotte Rogan, Chris and Mila Tewell and Gretchen Grant.

I am also indebted to my publisher, Laura Fillmore of Open Book Systems and Protean Press, and Laura's wonderful team— Karen Fuhrman, Janis Owens, Jenny Bennett, and Elizabeth Foz. Since Zoom cocktails with Cousin Lisa launched this writing project, it is only fitting that the editing and production process by Protean Press and its superb professionals was carried out in weekly Zoom meetings led by Karen.

The 2003 research and work of then graduate student Kirstie Jackson, Associate Member of Merton College Middle Common Room were indispensable to my understanding William Stoughton's bizarre notes about the "Evil Spirits" and how to make money. At the time she did the research, Kirstie was involved in various medieval and early modern projects for the University of Toronto, University of Reading, and King's College London. She was able to decipher and source the crabbed notes by William Stoughton on the rear flyleaf of *Select Discourses*. She did all of her research at the Bodleian Library Archives, at Oxford University where Stoughton studied and lived for more than a decade between his Harvard graduation in 1650 and his return to Massachusetts from Restoration England in 1662. The peerless Kirstie found a number of editions of Peacham's *The Worth Of A Penny*. She reported that the earliest edition is likely 1641, although it is possible there were earlier examples.

Finally, I am deeply indebted to my grandmother's Great-Aunt Ann and to Grandmother Brewster, the art student. I never knew either of them, but thanks to them, I know about Aunt Sally's clock and countless other bits of family lore from Wiscasset, Maine. I am very glad that they saved the Stoughton books and family papers, including the priceless 1797 letters to Rebecca, the girl with the sparkling eyes and alarming interest in parties. It is significant that Rebecca herself made the initial decision to save the letters written by her anxious mother, father, and older brother and sent to Rebecca while she was studying at Miss Druitt's in Boston. Rebecca brought the letters back with her from Boston and tucked them away in Wiscasset. Perhaps re-reading the letters made her smile or laugh or just remember how much her family cared. In any event, Rebecca treasured the urgent letters from her family, all so determined to protect her—in Judge Rice's words—from the "ruin of [her] innocence."

APPENDIX

The Appendix includes images of the title pages and flyleaves of three books that my brother Sam and I found in the steamer trunk in our family attic. The books were originally acquired by the Salem witchcraft judge, William Stoughton, when he was living in England between 1650 and 1662. In 1662 he fled England and returned to Massachusetts following Oliver Cromwell's death and the collapse of the Puritan Commonwealth. The books are in the order of their importance to the stories in this book:

Select Discourses; John Smith, London, 1660.

The True Doctrine of Justification Asserted & Vindicated from the Errours of Many, and more especially Papists and Socinians; Anthony Burgess, London, 1654.

A Cordial For A Fainting Soule; John Collings, London, 1652.

The eerie notes handwritten by Stoughton on the rear flyleaf of *Select Discourses* are seminal in the stories in *Witchcraft Legacy*.

Aspects of the other two Stoughton books reveal material of interest to me concerning both the witchcraft judge and the books' next owner, John Danforth.

Notably, *The True Doctrine*...displays Stoughton's and Danforth's names in different handwriting. William Stoughton's name is in a heavy pen stroke, consistent with his signatures on the death warrants in the Salem witchcraft trials and Stoughton's misogynistic and money-obsessed flyleaf notes in *Select Discourses*. Danforth's name is in a much thinner pen stroke.

Also of interest, Stoughton's notes on front flyleaf of *The True Doctrine...* record that he purchased the book from the library at New College, Oxford, for 4 shillings. Stoughton was pleased enough with the price to make a note of it on the flyleaf. It may be that his bargain purchase occurred after the 1660 Restoration when New College may have found it politically expedient to purge its shelves of Puritan religious tracts. Again, below Stoughton's name and notation, Danforth's name appears in his own distinctive and much finer pen stroke.

Danforth's pen strokes also appear elsewhere, including on the title page of *Select Discourses*, where he notes at the bottom of the page that the year of his birth (*"Anno nativitatis* John Danforth") was the same as the year of the book's publication (1660). Danforth was three decades younger than Stoughton.

The third book, *A Cordial For A Fainting Soule*, bears the names of Stoughton and Danforth on the top of the flyleaf, as well as notes written by, or relating to, a woman named Esther Willitt. I have been unable to identify Esther Willitt or piece together her untold story.

Finally, the Appendix includes Kirstie Jackson's transcription of the strange notations handwritten by Stoughton on the back flyleaf of *Select Discourses*.

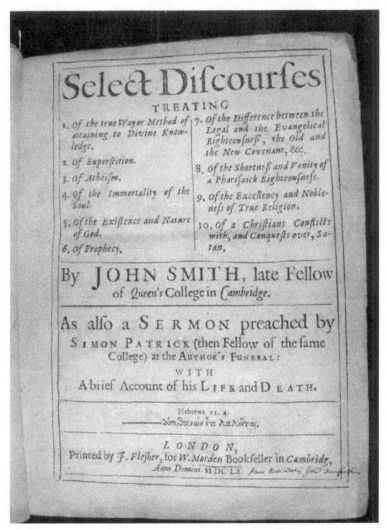

Title page from *Select Discourses*, John Smith, London, 1660.

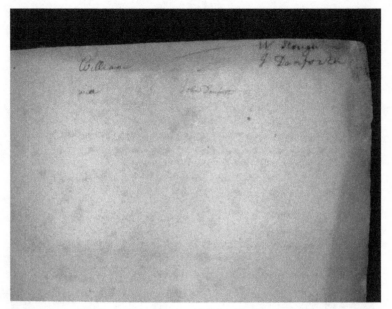

Signatures of William Stoughton and John Danforth, first and second
owners of *Select Discourses*; John Smith, London, 1660.

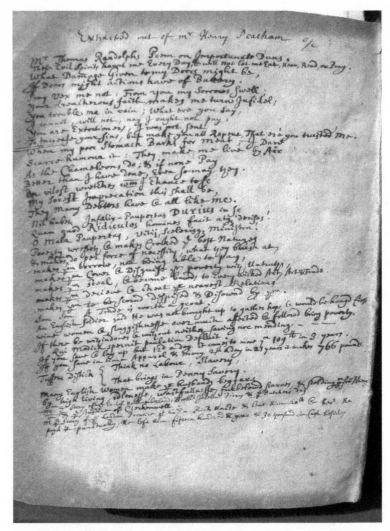

Handwritten notes "Extracted out of Mr. Henry Peacham" by William
Stoughton, chief judge of the Salem witchcraft trials, on the flyleaf of
Select Discourses; John Smith, London, 1660.

Extracted out of Mr Henry Peacham o/c:

Mr Thomas Randolph's Poem on Importunate Duns.

These Evil Spirits haunt me Every Day, & will not let me Eat, Hear, Read, or Pray.
What Damage Given to my Doors might be,
If Doors might actions have of Battery.
Pray Vex me not: From you my Sorrows Swell;
Your treacherous faith makes me turn Infidel;
You trouble me in vain; What ere you Say,
I cannot, will not, nay I ought not pay.
You are Extortioners, I was not Sent
To Increase your Sins, but make you all Repent, That er'e you trusted me.
Where my poor Stomach Barks for meat, I Dare
Scarce humour it: They make me live by Air
As the Chameleons do; & if none Pay
Better than I have done, Even so may they.
On vilest wretches whom I chance to se
My Sorest Imprecation this shall be,
They many Debtors have & all like me.
Nil habes Infælix – Paupertas DURIUS in se
Quam quod ridiculos hominess facit atque derisos!
O Mala Paupertas, Vitij, Scelerisque Ministra!
Poverty wresteth & makes Crooked ye best Natures
& makes them do per force of necessity, what they blush at,
makes them borrow, not being able to pay,
makes them Cover & Disguise their poverty with Untruths,
makes them steal, & become bawd, to Every wicked Act, Art & Trade.
makes them decieve & cheat their nearest Relations
makes them to be scorned despised & Disowned by them.
Son Son A Trade is worth a groat.
An English Soldier said He was not brought up to gather hops, & would be
    hangd first
Wine women & sluggishnesse over much affected & followd bring poverty.
If there be withindores & without neither saving nor mending - - -
    Qui Modica spernit paulatim Defluit.
If you Save & lay up but 12d a day it comes to more than 109li in 3 years.
If you Save in time Apparel & Mony 2sh a day in 21 years it makes 766 pounds.
Tuffers Distick   Think no Labour, Slavery.
                That brings in Penny Savery.
Many English Women make their husbands beggars
By high living, idlenesse, wastfullnesse, furbelowd Scarves, & scolding them
    from Home
Mem.: ye story of ye Earl of Northumberland, Brother Jocelen Peirs & ye Butchers
    dog
Mem.: & ye Justice of Clerkenwell.
Mem.: ye Story of ye London Prentice yat had a Rich Uncle & lent Him 20li
    & because, He
Payd it punctually, He left Him fifteen hundred a year & 30 thousand in Cash
    besides.

Transcribed by Kirstie Jackson

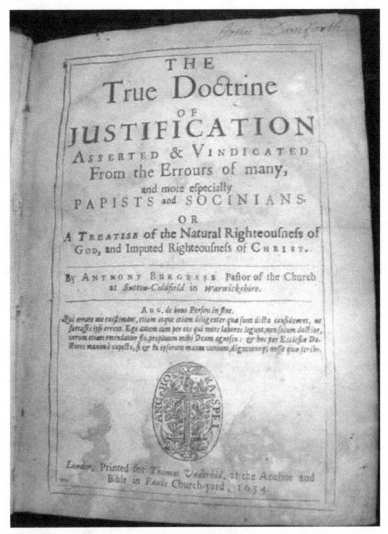

Title page (with John Danforth's signature in the top righthand
corner) of *The True Doctrine of Justification Asserted & Vindicated from
the Errours of Many, and more especially Papists and Socinians*; Anthony
Burgess, London, 1654.

Flyleaf with signatures of William Stoughton and John Danforth, first and second owners of *The True Doctrine of Justification*; Anthony Burgess, London, 1654, including Stoughton's note that he purchased the book for 4 shillings from New College, Oxford.

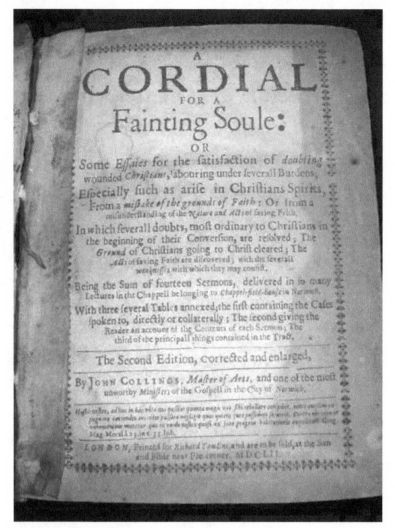

Title page from *A Cordial For A Fainting Soule*, John Collings, London, 1652.

Note of (or relating to) Esther Willitt on the inside cover of *A Cordial For A Fainting Soule*; John Collings, London, 1652.

Inside cover—with signatures of William Stoughton and John Danforth—of *A Cordial For A Fainting Soule* (John Collings, London, 1652).

BIBLIOGRAPHY

Either I or Kirstie Jackson, my wonderful researcher at the Bodleian Library Archives, Oxford, found some of the material listed below. Kirstie's research and the other sources listed below helped me flesh out the stories in *Witchcraft Legacy* to the extent those stories do not come straight out of my own experience or out of the steamer trunk in the attic of the Big House.

Allen, Charles Edwin. *History of Dresden Maine.* Lewiston, Maine: Twin City Printery, 1931.

Brewster, Isabel Erskine. *Recollections.* Concord, NH: Rumford Press, 1934.

Burgess, Anthony. *The True Doctrine of Justification Asserted and Vindicated From the Errours of many and more especially Papists and Socinians.* London: 1654. (Purchased by William Stoughton from the New College, Oxford, library for 4 shillings—"pr. 4d," i.e. *pretio* 4d, or price 4 shillings.)

Collings, John. *A Cordial For A Fainting Soul.* London: 1652.

Cook, Clarence, ed. *A Girl's Life Eighty Years Ago,* Selections from the Letters of Eliza Southgate Bowne. New York: Charles Scribner's Sons, 1887.

Hazlitt, W. Carew, ed. *Political and Dramatic Works of Thomas Randolph, Vol. II,* pp. 633–636. London: Reeves and Turner, 1875. (Kirstie Jackson reports that in the Hazlitt compilation she found the identical [and additional] verses of the Randolph poem, "Those Evil Spirits…" as quoted on the flyleaf of Stoughton's copy of *Select Discourses.* The Randolph poem, located by Kirstie in the Bodleian Archives, is entitled "Mr. Randolph's Petition to his Creditors." Randolph is much better known for his poem, "Stolen sweets are always sweeter…" which appears in the *Oxford Book Of English Verse.*)

Laplante, Eve. *Salem Witch Judge, The Life and Repentence of Samuel Sewall.* New York: HarperOne, a division of HarperCollins, 2007.

Orcutt, William Dana. *Good Old Dorchester, A Narrative History Of The Town 1630–1893.* Cambridge, MA: John Wilson & Son, University Press, 1893.

Salem Witchcraft Papers, http://salem.lib.virginia.edu/home.html

Schiff, Stacy. *The Witches, Salem, 1692.* New York: Little Brown and Company, 2015.

Smith, John. *Select Discourses.* London: 1660.

Stephen, Leslie, Sydney Lee, Sir, George Smith. *The Dictionary of National Biography*, "Biography of William Stoughton." London: Oxford University Press, 1973.

Tusser, Thomas. *The Ladder to Thrift, Five Hundred Points of Good Husbandrie.* London: 1580.

CPSIA information can be obtained
at www.ICGtesting.com
Printed in the USA
LVHW040240190522
719082LV00003B/474